Urban Green

Urban Green

Innovative Parks for Resurgent Cities

Peter Harnik

**ISLAND**PRESS

Washington | Covelo | London

ISLAND PRESS is a trademark of the Center for Resource Economics.

Library of Congress Cataloging-in-Publication Data

Harnik, Peter.
  Urban green : innovative parks for resurgent cities /
Peter Harnik.
     p.   cm.
  Includes bibliographical references and index.
  ISBN-13: 978-1-59726-679-6 (cloth : alk. paper)
  ISBN-10: 1-59726-679-5 (cloth : alk. paper)
  ISBN-13: 978-1-59726-684-0 (pbk. : alk. paper)
  ISBN-10: 1-59726-684-1 (pbk. : alk. paper)
  1. Urban parks—United States. 2. City planning—United States.
3. Open spaces—United States. 4. Urban renewal—United States.
5. Urban landscape architecture—United States. I. Title.
  SB482.A4H35 2010
  712'.50973—dc22   2009043096

Printed using Times New Roman
Text design and Typesetting by Paul Hotvedt, Blue Heron Typesetting

Printed on recycled, acid-free paper

Manufactured in the United States of America
10   9   8   7   6   5   4   3   2

Keywords: urban parks, park planning and design, urban redevelopment,
community gardens, landfills, wetlands and stormwater sewage ponds, rail
trails, green roofs, schoolyard parks, covered resevoirs, river and stream
corridors, cemetary parks, boulevards and parkways, decked highways,
removing parking

*To Andrew and Rebecca
and their up-and-coming generation*

Contents

TABLES

Foreword

For city residents the world over, public parks hold a special place in our hearts. They're our backyards, our country escapes, our athletic facilities, our beaches, and our nature preserves all rolled into one. They are places where families from every imaginable background come together and share in the sense of community that is at the heart of city life. Parks help clean the air we breathe, reduce carbon emissions, attract businesses and tourists, and provide a home for cultural celebrations and events. And for city kids, parks are living classrooms where the natural world comes alive.

Few would dispute that parks bring all these benefits and more to urban residents. But in most cities, including New York, space is at a premium—and so the question is not *should* we create more parks and public spaces, but *how* do we do it? In this book, Peter Harnik examines cities around the country that are facing this very challenge and finding creative solutions. He reveals how the push to preserve and promote our nation's urban parks is one of the most exciting frontiers in urban planning, dramatically changing the way we think about what is possible in a twenty-first-century city.

Here in New York City, where undeveloped land is scarce, we have worked hard to expand our 29,000 acres of public parkland by reclaiming areas from decades of industrial neglect. From the new Brooklyn Bridge Park to the East River Park in Manhattan and the Bronx River greenway, we're reconnecting communities to one of our most precious assets: the waterfront. On Staten Island, we've begun converting the city's old landfill into a 2,000-acre park that will be nothing short of spectacular. And in West Chelsea, we've used innovative designs to transform an abandoned elevated rail track into a beautiful walkway with stunning city views.

All told, New York City has added more than 500 acres of new parkland over the last eight years—the largest parks expansion program since President Franklin D. Roosevelt's Works Progress Administration of the 1930s. Our goal is for every New Yorker to live within a ten-minute walk of a public park, but we also recognize that expanding our parkland is not enough. Creating a truly green city requires finding creative ways to bring some of the benefits of public parks to private places. That's why we've incentivized green roofs through tax abatements, supported community gardens, and opened school playgrounds to the community during after-school hours and on weekends. We've also teamed with Bette Midler and the New York Restoration Project to launch *MillionTreesNYC*, through which we'll plant and care for 1 million new trees over the next ten years. Two years into the program, we are well ahead of our planting goals.

All of this work is at the heart of *PlaNYC*, our long-term sustainability plan that will allow us to create a greener, greater New York. Achieving its ambitious goals—including cutting the city's carbon emissions by 30 percent by the year 2030—will require not only a sustained commitment from city government, but also two valuable resources that every city has at its disposal: volunteerism and public-private partnerships.

Each year in New York City, more than 800 groups and 55,000 people pitch in to help beautify and preserve our parks. To encourage even more New Yorkers to get involved in their communities, and to answer President Obama's call for a new era of volunteerism, we recently introduced *NYC Service*. The program is helping us to drive volunteers to our areas of greatest need, including environmental protection. At the same time, we've expanded our use of public-private partnership to improve our parks. *MillionTreesNYC* is just one example of how we have enlisted the support of private organizations to expand and support our parks. Without private support, the High Line Park would never have been created, and the elevated rail line would likely have been torn down.

As we search for new ways to make our city greener than ever, we are not shy about borrowing the best and most exciting new ideas from other cities—and you'll find many of them inside this book. As Peter Harnik expertly demonstrates, the urban park is as fertile ground for fresh new thinking as it is for the plants and trees that clean our air and improve our lives. As some of these ideas take root in your own mind, I hope you'll work with leaders in your own communities to help create the next generation of great urban parks. Together, we can build a greener, healthier future for our cities and everyone who calls them home.

—Michael R. Bloomberg, Mayor
New York, New York
December 2009

Acknowledgments

Any book that relies on factual research, group experiences, and personal anecdotes grows out of the collective wisdom and narratives of scores of people, especially a book that tries to pull together new thinking in a field that has been understudied and underdocumented for years. Naturally, all the conclusions, analyses, predictions, and errors are mine alone—but I am deeply indebted to a vast army of urban experts, park managers, advocates, and park enthusiasts from around the nation who helped with data, insight, and opinions. Most central to this enterprise was Ben Welle, assistant director of the Center for City Park Excellence, without whose research, writing, and thoughtfulness this book could not have been written and to whom I am most appreciative. Special thanks also go to The Trust for Public Land and its president, Will Rogers, for generously supporting my hours "off the grid" while the book was being written and revised. Thanks also to my outstanding editor at Island Press, Heather Boyer.

In addition, I want to thank, in no order other than alphabetical, my many friends and collaborators, new and old, who assisted in so many ways: Bond Anderson, Susan Baird, Thomas Balsley, Janet Bebb, Vicki Been, Charles Beveridge, Gia Biaggi, Marti Bjornson, Kathy Blaha, Stephanie Bothwell, Charles Brecher, David Brewster, Dave Canaan, Phil Carpenter, Ethan Carr, Jeff Ciabotti, Jerry Cole, Luci Correa, Lois Cortel, John Crompton, Andrew Dannenberg, Will deBoer, Lara deSouza, Rick Dewees, Kathy Dickhut, Rich Dolesh, Susan Donaldson, Jim Dowell, Andrew du Moulin, Woody Duncan, George Dusenbury, Paul Dyer, Ted Eisenman, Peter Ellsworth, Caryn Ernst, Mary Eysenbach, Gary Fichter, Lois Finkelman, Richard Foot, Mark Fusco, Jim Garges, Alex Garvin, Coleen Gentles, Geoffrey Godbey, Peggy Greenwell, Deb Guenther, Dana Gumb, James Hall, Dianne Harnell-Cohen, Rebecca Harnik, Robbie Hilstonsmith, Mark Hinshaw, Stanley Ivan, Jane Jacobs, Destry Jarvis, Larry Kaplan, Noah Kaufman, Liam Kavanagh, Kevin Kuharic, Daniel Laforte, Dale Larsen, Laura Lawson, Mary Alice Lee, Jack Linn, David Little, Joe Mathers, Rich McDonald, Mark McHenry, Aric Merolli, Norman Merrifield, Timothy Mitchell, Greg Mitterman, David Moore, Jon Kirk Mukri, Tom Murphy, Catherine Nagel, Mark Oliver, Anne Olson, Kathleen Ownby, Neal Peirce,

Tom Phillips, Catherine Pickering, Leslie Pohl-Kosbau, Dewey Potter, Marion Pressley, Karla Price, Nathaniel Reed, Reid Reiner, Breece Robertson, Zari Santner, Jim Sargen, Bob Schwartz, Joe Sehee, Scott Shafer, Chris Shaheen, Leah Shahum, Michael Shiosaki, Dan Skillman, Andy Stone, Michael Taylor, Tupper Thomas, Joe Turner, Tom van Buskirk, Andrew Vesselinovich, Isabel Wade, Beth White, and Brett Wright.

Finally, I want to thank my wife, Carol Parker, for putting up with the loss of so many nights and weekends to the flickering computer screen—I will now atone by taking you and the dog for long walks in the park.

🌱 🌱 🌱

Portions of this book appeared in different forms in *Journal of Housing and Community Development; Landscape Architecture; Places Forum for the Design of the Public Realm; Planning; Parks and Recreation;* and *Urban Land.*

Introduction

For more than half a century, beginning right after World War II, the United States engaged in a mammoth experiment about a new way to live on the land. Using the automobile, the highway, a heavy dose of energy, and fantastic sums of money we redesigned our cities as sprawling, low-density metropolitan areas with segregated functions, multiple nodes, and, often, no dominant center. New cities were laid out from scratch using this unprecedented auto-based template; old cities were heavy-handedly reworked to make their earlier pattern fit a prodigious number of cars. For a while the experiment seemed a success—not only did it get many people into detached houses surrounded by lawns but it also coincided with the period of U.S. economic, political, and military global dominance. Recently the experiment has started to appear a failure. It turns out that we drained the planet of vast quantities of fuel, helped to alter the atmosphere in perhaps devastating ways, paved over too much farm- and forestland, and in the process surprised ourselves by becoming seriously overweight.

Fortunately the pendulum has started its return swing. Cities are reasserting their centrality, and urbanophiles are again able to extol such values as walkability and mixed uses that had been scorned by planners for decades. There is a rise in new leaders who respect, care about, and even love cities—committed and visionary mayors, developers, entrepreneurs, neighborhood activists, academics, and others. Mass transit and transit-oriented development are again taken seriously—as are other collective enterprises, such as green spaces for all. With the rebirth of the city has come the rebirth of the city park.

Now that parks are back on the public's agenda, now that cities are vying with one another for "best park system" and the "livability crown," now that park advocates are being invited to important planning meetings instead of picketing them on the outside, what exactly should we be doing? The first half of the answer is, if not easy, at least obvious and quite well documented: fix up the existing parks. Follow the lead of the Central Park Conservancy, Philadelphia Green, Washington Parks and People, Seattle Parks Foundation, Detroit River Conservancy, and scores of other groups who are turning old parks from "poor" to "good" and from "good" to "great." The second half of

1

the answer—what this book is about—is creating more urban natural spaces and people places.

Cities are extraordinarily complicated and intricate. As we learned from the devastating impact of highway construction, that intricacy requires respect and even humility. Urban space is highly contested; every potential new park is in competition with many other uses, most of which are powerfully driven by cost-benefit analyses and the profit motive. Parks add value to neighborhoods, but neighborhoods also add value to parks, so the development of the two must go hand in hand. This book shows numerous realistic solutions, from reusing the land under defunct factories to sharing schoolyards, from building trails on abandoned tracks to planting community gardens, from decking parks over highways to allowing more activities in cemeteries, from eliminating parking lots to uncovering buried streams, and more. No strategy alone is perfect, and each, in fact, has its own set of realities. Collectively they suggest a path toward making modern cities softer, more beautiful, more sociable, more fun, more ecologically sound, and more successful.

This book also deals with the human side of the equation. After years of hand-wringing, protesting, and even losing faith, city park advocates are finding themselves on a radically changed playing field. We must rethink our strategies, relearn what is involved in having a seat at the table, and in some cases change our tone. Being a player means supporting positions with documentable facts and figures, marshalling supporters, reaching out to others, and compromising when necessary. That's the other message here—it is time now to rely less on pro forma standards and more on the political give-and-take of real life in the city. This book highlights dozens of hard-fought successes and shows how getting anything done for the public domain requires leaders and activists with unusual creativity, stamina, and political skills.

❦   ❦   ❦

Many Americans have heard great tales about our national parks: John Wesley Powell, with only one arm, leading an exploration in wooden boats down the Colorado River through the Grand Canyon; or John Muir alerting the world to the glory of Yosemite; or Supreme Court Justice William O. Douglas leading eighteen consecutive annual hikes along the abandoned C&O Canal—the first with five compatriots, the last with 50,000—in order to thwart its planned destruction by the highway builders; or the Rockefeller family donating much of the land to create not only the Great Smoky Mountains National Park but also Acadia, the Grand Tetons, the Redwoods, and the Virgin Islands National Parks.

Many people don't realize that there are stories just as good—or better—about our city parks, those wonderful patches of green that we've got right in our midst day in and day out.

Stories, for instance, about Frederick Law Olmsted, who codesigned Central Park in New York City and also oversaw its construction. Millions of mothers may tell their children that Central Park is what New York looked like before all the buildings, but actually the park was created and is about as natural as Disneyland. In fact, with the enormous amount of rock excavation, earth moving, tree planting, water diversion, and physical construction, it was the largest public works project in U.S. history at that time. Later, Olmsted, who had literally created the field of landscape architecture, went one step further and created the field of landscape economics. He was the first person to hypothesize that the taxes from the increased real estate value generated from Central Park would be greater than the cost of the park. It was an incredible concept, one that even today most people do not understand or recognize. However, he was right. The New Parks Commission in New York City, writing ten years after the opening of Central Park, said:

> While the property in the other nineteen wards of the city increased but twofold, the property of the three wards in which Central Park was located advanced from about $26.5 millions to over $312 millions. Whereas before the making of the park, these three wards paid one dollar in every thirteen received as taxes, after the making of the park they paid one-third of the entire expenses of the city and this notwithstanding the fact that the taking of the ground for Central Park removed 10,000 lots from tax books of the city.

A less well-known hero was Edward Bigelow, public works director in Pittsburgh in the late 1800s, who rescued the estate of Mary Schenley from the clutches of a housing developer by surreptitiously boarding the very same night-train and the very same steamship to London and racing by carriage to ask the wealthy heiress to donate her 400 acres before his competitor could make a financial offer. And Bigelow had the nerve to try this ploy barely a month after the people of Pittsburgh had voted down a $3 million bond issue to buy the land off her. She graciously agreed, and the property today is Schenley Park.

In San Francisco, Golden Gate Park had a wonderful superintendent in John McLaren, a flinty Scotsman who served for fifty-six years and who responded to his workers' complaints about not being given jackets against the chilly fog with, "Anyone who is cold isn't working hard enough." When a traction trolley company bullied the city council into issuing a permit to cross his park, McLaren thwarted the effort by having gardeners work all night planting a pathway of rhododendrons eight feet wide directly in the planned route of the train. Because of his legendary hatred of city-approved park statues, he always ordered the planting of trees in front of each new one. McLaren, who created his paradise out of seemingly worthless shifting sands, was so beloved that in 1917 he was exempted from mandatory retirement. He lived another twenty-six years, dying in his office at the age of ninety-six.

The stories aren't only about historical places and dead people. Chicago's Mayor Richard M. Daley, once mocked by the local press as the "Petunia Mayor" for his beautification efforts, has turned his city into a poster for the equation that refinement plus livability equals economic vitality. Now reporters are asking, "How did he know?" Story has it that Daley got the idea for Millennium Park while looking at the ugly open railroad tracks from the window of his dentist's office high above Michigan Avenue. "Let's see what can be done," he said, and rarely have six little words had such an impact on a city.

Or consider the recent mayor of Pittsburgh, Tom Murphy, son of a steelworker and a fierce advocate for trails. With its many defunct steel mills, Pittsburgh had more miles of spectacular, unreachable riverfront than almost anyplace else. Murphy, whose motto seems to be, "What good is a river if you can't run alongside it?" vowed when he was elected in 1994 that nothing new would be built riverside without leaving space for people. Soon thereafter PNC Corp. unveiled plans for a spectacular new headquarters on the Monongahela River. Everyone breathed a sigh of relief that the big bank wasn't moving to the suburbs. Not Murphy. The Mayor asked the company president to pull the building back 50 feet and leave space for a trail. "You've got to be kidding!" was the response, but today the bank has a trail and a trailside entranceway and is a national leader in bike commuting and midday jogging. A few miles upriver, the University of Pittsburgh and the Pittsburgh Steelers had selected their optimum spot for four practice football fields. The trouble was, the site went right down to the river's edge. When the smoke cleared, the mayor had his riverfront trail and the Steelers had four gleaming practice football fields that are only 80 yards long.

National parks may guard and highlight the totemic landscapes and stories of the nation, but city parks are where we spend most of our park time—toddling as babies, competing as children, hanging out as teens, courting, bringing families, taking visitors, and sitting on benches when exhausted. We go *to* them, walk *through* them, look *at* them, dream *of* them. And the greatest, from Balboa Park in San Diego to Forest Park in St. Louis to Fairmount Park in Philadelphia, often become the very symbols of their cities, the central touchstones of memory and experience for residents and tourists alike.

From coast to coast America's cities are today on an upward trajectory. Some, like Chandler, Arizona, are in their very first growth cycle. Others, like Atlanta, are bouncing back from years of decline. Even cities, like Cleveland, that are not on the path of full recovery have sections and neighborhoods that are seeing revival and an overall urban picture that has many reasons for hope. Parks have played—and will play—a significant role in this good fortune. Cities are enormous and intricate economic engines, but ultimately they are creatures of human free will and respond to people's desires for livable environments. While mankind cannot do much about the brutal winter of the Twin Cities, the rain of Seattle, or the blistering heat of Phoenix, people can create (and have created) great park systems in those and other locations to help mitigate the drawbacks and embellish on the strengths. Other cities are continually pushed to meet and exceed their competition or they begin to lose out. That challenge is met by parks as much as, or more than, any other amenity.

A major problem for advocates and managers is that parks *seem* relatively simple and straightforward. In fact, they are immensely complicated. People frequently say, "It's not rocket science, it's just a park." Or, "If you think parks are tough, you should see how difficult highways are." No! For rockets and highways you need to be good at math. Parks require math plus horticulture, hydrology, psychology, sociology, and communication. If you want proof, go to any freeway onramp and look at the sign: "This Is a Limited Access Highway—No Hitchhiking,

Pedestrians, Bicycles, Farm Equipment, Animal-Drawn Vehicles, Push-Carts," and so on and so forth. If it doesn't fit their parameters, they ban it. You can't do that with a park.

Even the preeminent urbanist Jane Jacobs, who loved great parks, realized what a wrenching challenge they can be. Writing in *The Death and Life of Great American Cities*, she said:

> Parks are volatile places. They tend to run to extremes of popularity and unpopularity. Their behavior is far from simple. They can be delightful features of city districts, and economic assets to their surroundings as well, but pitifully few are. They can grow more beloved and valuable with the years, but pitifully few show this staying power. For every Rittenhouse Square in Philadelphia, or Rockefeller Plaza or Washington Square in New York, or Boston Common, or their loved equivalents in other cities, there are dozens of dispirited city vacuums called parks, eaten around with decay, little used, unloved.

Jacobs was writing in 1961 as American cities were finishing their first decade of the steep decline that engulfed most of them for the rest of the century. Today the tide seems to be turning for many, but the lessons and caveats that arose during that bleak period bear watching and considering as a new round of park-building gets underway.

🐾 🐾 🐾

In January 1954, in an orange grove far outside Los Angeles, ground was broken for Disneyland. Fifty years later, in July 2004, on top of a rail yard in the heart of Chicago, the ribbon was cut for Millennium Park. Halfway between those two events, in December 1980 in New York City, the Central Park Conservancy was incorporated. Three very different cities, three momentous occurrences; together they may well serve as the urban park cultural brackets of the Baby Boom generation.

From the moment Disneyland opened it became the new paradigm of a park experience—corporate, programmed, extravagant, rural, flawless, and electrifying. It was not a coincidence that after Disneyland opened, the old urban park systems—unprogrammed, democratic, unpredictable, and free—began grinding down relentlessly everywhere from Franklin Park in Boston to Golden Gate Park in San Francisco. There was something completely new in the air and it was exciting: the park experience could be sanitized! Social classes could be segregated! Suburban backyards would meet most of the old city park needs, and Disneyland—or the concept of Disneyland—would pick up the rest.

By 2004 those original Disneyland children had gray hair, aching backs, and worn-out knees. The thrill of spending $400 for a family trip to an amusement park had faded. The suburban backyard was becoming a hassle and the stairs to the second floor tedious. An apartment downtown seemed intriguing, particularly if it was near . . . that fabulous new Millennium Park. No thrill rides (thank God!), but their more mature equivalents: eye-popping sculpture, wonderful fountains, concerts every week, a sumptuous garden that changed with the seasons, theater, bicycle parking, ice-skating in the winter (do you think we can still skate?), two restaurants, a serpentine bridge that wowed visiting relatives, a constant stream of interesting humanity to watch, and, finally, a sense of being back in the center of things.

Meanwhile, back in New York, where the city park movement had initially ignited in the 1860s, Central Park was the scene of a different and highly un-American kind of experiment—the unprecedented attempt not to replace an old icon but to gloriously refurbish it. Beginning with wealthy and influential park neighbors looking out for their own safety, views, and property values, the conservancy evolved into a sophisticated and admired spouse of the city parks department, seemingly knowing every step of the complicated dance that is the daily relationship between a city and its greatest park.

Millennium Park exploded onto the urban scene with an impact not felt since Central Park was unveiled. Central Park itself clawed its way back from urban embarrassment to civic Cinderella over a period of several decades. In both cases, the price tag approached half a billion dollars. In both cases, the metropolitan effect—from property value to tourism to unforgettableness and civic pride to just plain fun—was priceless. Today it is close to unimaginable for a tourist visiting either city not to sample those parks. Even more significant, the buzz is affecting other places, too. Stunning new parks have opened in Boston, Atlanta, Houston, St. Louis, Cincinnati, Santa Fe, and Denver, and extraordinarily successful conservancies have been revamping great old parks in Pittsburgh, St. Louis, Brooklyn, San Francisco, Atlanta, and Houston. Frankly, there is hardly a city worth its salt not considering some kind of new or revamped green gathering spot around which to design a swinging downtown. Disneyland technically might still be fun, but that paradigm no longer rules.

🌹 🌹 🌹

With cities returning to centrality—with the metropolitan doughnut becoming whole again—it is time to rediscover and reestablish the proper way to plan for urban parks. This art is not new, but it was lost for many years. Park thinking was remarkably sophisticated and robust back in the 1920s and earlier, and it can be rediscovered and amplified. The key is to return to considerations that were forgotten or ignored in the din of suburbanization and sprawl: human scale, walkability, efficiency, and respect for ecological principles and democratic ideals. Parks, ultimately, are an interplay—a conversation, if you will—between people and nature. After a many-year hiatus, it is time to restart this conversation at a basic level: How much parkland do we want in our cities, and where can we put what we want?

Part I of this book reviews the history of urban park planning and shows how we got to where we are today. It also sets forth a comprehensive and inclusive procedure whereby everyone in a community can participate in the discussion of what should happen.

Part II turns to the reality issue: what land opportunities are available for cities that have gone through the planning process and find themselves short of parks? This is where we move from elaborate theoretical tapestries to the hard reality of finding feasible locations for creating parks: *How does a city actually get more parkland?*

When cities are young and expanding, parks are added on the leading edge of the growth margin. They consist of natural lands—farms, forests, woodlands, wetlands, deserts, and other relatively undeveloped properties that are donated or purchased for park use. Often the trees and other plant materials can be retained, and little or no demolition is required. Sometimes, no construction is required, either. The process is known as *conservation,* and it's relatively easy, straightforward, and comprehensible.

But in older, "all built out" cities, there is nothing natural to conserve—there is no remaining nature aside from the existing parks. Creating any new park involves *development* rather than conservation. A derelict parking lot, for instance, that might make a great new park wouldn't be *conserved*—doing that would merely retain a derelict parking lot. It would be torn up, regraded, planted, and fitted out with a playground or a sports field or a fountain or whatever the community wants. Development is less straightforward and tends to be less comprehensible to the average citizen because it can take so many different forms: acquiring no-longer-needed parcels from other government agencies, sharing land, providing rules or incentives that encourage developer donations, using previously unused surfaces like rooftops, or making better use of existing parkland. All of these approaches will be discussed in the second part of the book.

If there are any unifying threads to these techniques, they are creativity, a willingness to experiment, and a willingness to compromise. Many of them also require money—usually more money than would be spent for a similar amount of acreage in a less congested rural or suburban environment. Building on a rooftop, for instance, is more costly than building on the ground—except that ground prices downtown are often impossibly exorbitant. Developing a park on an old landfill has numerous expenses that don't come into play on regular earth—except that regular earth downtown just isn't available. Conversely, some solutions—such as those that involve sharing school, roadway, or cemetery land—can actually save money by relying on multiple funding sources. At the same time, the value created is so much higher. New York City's diminutive Bryant Park, six acres among a forest of skyscrapers near Times Square, is "needed" by many more people than a comparably sized suburban or rural enclave of trees and grass. That need can be demonstrated by, among other things, the collective willingness to pay for the park's $3.5 million annual budget.

The biggest problem in cities involves not so much the land as the people—the large numbers of persons who have other ideas, other missions, and other opinions. Mothers who initially don't like the idea of schoolyards being open to adult strangers after school hours. Building custodians who initially worry that a rooftop park could damage the water resistance of the ceiling membrane. Highway engineers who are initially convinced that a tree-filled parkway median will lead to accidents. Stormwater engineers who initially swear that park-based natural systems will lead to more flooding. Railroad companies that initially believe they have legal liability to remove all bridges before abandoning a rail line.

Though none of these challenges is insurmountable, all of them are real. Each has to be taken seriously and solved legally, financially, or politically—which is why many of these innovative projects take years to accomplish. But every concept in this book has been proven at least once, in at least one community, and each success makes the next attempt easier and more likely to succeed.

PART I

Of Cities and Parks

CHAPTER I

How Much Parkland Should a City Have?

"Does my city have enough parkland?" "How about bike trails?" "What is the farthest any resident should be from a park?" "How can I keep our soccer moms and our tree huggers from killing each other?" "My neighborhood has no parks—how do I get one?" "How much natural land do we need for stormwater retention?" "We have a very nice park that almost no one uses—what's wrong?"

If you run something called the Center for City Park Excellence, these kinds of queries roll in like waves in a wave pool. They are asked by reporters, academics, and the public at large. They are asked by park officials and they're asked by mayors.

Until the 1920s there were few answers to these questions. In fact, the questions weren't asked. Parks were such a wondrous new phenomenon, and they were so rare, that the goal was to get as many as possible. It was similar to America's attitude toward highways in the 1950s and jails in the 1990s—there almost couldn't be enough. But beginning in the 1930s, popular enthusiasm for urban parks began to slacken. More exciting things were in the air. For one, there were scores of awe-inspiring national parks coming on line, from the Everglades, Acadia, and the Great Smokies to Isle Royale, Big Bend, and Saguaro. For another, the movement to suburbs had begun and more people—influential people, taxpaying people—suddenly had yards. Even though yards didn't fulfill even one-tenth the many roles of parks, they *seemed* like little green parks. And it seemed redundant to pay a mortgage for a private yard and then pay taxes for a public park. (While there was a brief urban park resurgence with Civilian Conservation Corps projects during the Depression, that was, after all, a federally funded make-work program.) Beginning as a slight desiccation in the 1930s and then a drought following the Depression, after World War II the political will for city parks virtually dried up.

With the rug pulled out from under them, the reduced cadre of urban park advocates was put on the defensive. Needing to devise a substitute for the former grassroots momentum, they sought to erect a formalistic planning structure. To stave off a full-scale reversal, they created an apparently scientific scheme to replace the previous hurly-burly of political action. When asked how much parkland a city should have, park experts said 10 acres for every 1,000 persons. There were similarly official answers for other questions such as miles of multiuse trail (one for every 8,000 persons), picnic tables (ten to fifteen per acre), even the amount of sailing space (one acre of water for every four sailboats). It was as if it had come from the Bible: "And on the eighth day, God created a 100-acre district park with a service area radius of 5 miles, and he saw that it was good." This scientific prescriptionism continued for more than two generations, all the way into the 1990s.

There was only one problem. It didn't work for real cities. The amount of parkland that cities *did* have and the amount that they *should have had* bore no relation to each other (see table 1.1). Chicago, despite being home to the American Planning Association, is notably short of parkland. Jacksonville, located in a gargantuan marsh, is so far over any kind of prescribed standard that it would have to have sell off tens of thousands of protected acres or bring in millions of more residents to get *down* to the standard. In fact, over the years, crowded Chicago has barely made a dent in its parkland deficit while sprawling Jacksonville has continued to amass acreage that is hardly ever visited by a living human being.

This is not to criticize either Chicago or Jacksonville, each of which has a unique and outstanding park, recreation, and conservation program. But it is to make the case that standards do not a great park system make.

It is politics that makes a great park system—politics based on the muscle of grassroots support, the brains of sophisticated leadership, and the nerves of elected politicians who know when to stand firm and when to compromise. This kind of politics—the kind that created the great early park systems in Boston, Baltimore, Buffalo, Cleveland, Minneapolis, and other places—cannot be replaced by standards. It is this kind of politics that U.S. cities must return to if they are to use parks

Table 1.1 That's Quite a Spread You've Got!
Acres of Parkland per 1,000 Persons, Selected Cites

City	Population	Park Acres	Acres per 1,000 Persons
Jacksonville	805,605	46,241	57.4
Albuquerque	518,271	34,630	66.8
Raleigh	375,806	12,252	32.6
Oakland	401,489	5,217	13.0
Chicago	2,836,658	11,860	4.2
Santa Ana	339,555	357	1.1

Source: Center for City Park Excellence, The Trust for Public Land

for all their benefits: promoting weight loss and healthy living, adding beauty, strengthening the urban core, limiting suburban sprawl, protecting the environment, and even fighting global warming.

In some situations, such as in rapidly urbanizing rural areas under the control of a few large builders, hard-and-fast standards may work. Because of the availability of land, some standards are even feasible, assuming skillful planning and strong government regulations. The Phoenix park system grew up almost entirely after the time of old-fashioned park enthusiasm and during the period of standards (Phoenix didn't reach a population of 100,000 until 1949), and it's a large and successful system. But even there it seems that politics played a bigger role than may be obvious. Nearby cities Mesa and Tucson, which also came of age during the "standards era," have small and less inspired systems. It wasn't just the standards that worked in Phoenix, it was the politics that propelled allegiance to them.

But in already-developed urban areas it is much tougher. Most of these recommended standards are unattainable. Holding them up as a goal serves only to make city park agencies look incompetent. There are far too many existing structures, streets, uses, patterns, customs, expectations, and general history to plop down new one-size-fits-all parks or to meet a dry mathematical formula in existing cities. The only way to strengthen an urban park system is to strengthen the political constituency promoting it.

In the 1930s, New York City Parks Commissioner Robert Moses said, "There is no such thing as a fixed percentage of park area to population. . . . Sensible, practical people know that [it] depends upon the actual problems of the city in question." Alexander Garvin, in his book *The American City: What Works, What Doesn't,* addresses the fruitlessness of the rigid acres-per-thousand approach when applied to true urban areas:

> In 1943, the American Society of Planning Officials proposed lowering the standard to 10 acres for every 3,000 city residents in cities with populations above 1 million, because higher standards were not attainable in more densely populated areas. The absurdity of this numbers game eluded them, too. At a standard of 10 acres per 1,000 population, Manhattan at its peak population of 2,331,542 in 1910 would have required 23,315 acres of park, more than the island's entire 14,870 acres. Even at ASPO's lower standard . . . half of Manhattan would have to have been set aside for parkland.

The most recent efforts to set a standard for the "correct" amount of parkland in a city were made through the auspices of the National Recreation and Park Association in 1971, 1983, and 1995. Each one entailed great amounts of work—the 160-page 1995 book took three years to complete. Unfortunately, each was carried out in a special kind of data vacuum. While the research professionals were the best and brightest in the parks and recreation fields, they were only modestly attuned to the complexities of urban life. They had the most comprehensive data on how many adults would swim if a pool was within a particular distance or how many children could be served by an average-sized playground, but there was no context. True-to-life data about true-to-life cities were not in the picture: housing types, zoning laws, transit (or the lack thereof), waterways, street widths, bike lanes, parking requirements, railyards, shopping districts, school locations, festivals, highways, wealth distribution, crime, language, culture. Parks represent only one "silo" out of dozens of intertwined factors that make up a city, yet those other silos have a significant impact on the need, design, and use of parks.

To be fair, none of us can fully comprehend the complexity of the urban labyrinth. It may be possible to construct something visually pleasing with evenly spaced green polygons on a color-coded map or to arrange artful golf courses in a "simulated city" computer game, but real-life cities have too many physical impediments, political interferences, and cultural and economic exceptionalities for simple standards to rule. Venice, Italy, is 700 years old and widely considered to be a wonderfully successful and inviting city, yet it has a miniscule number of trees, no traditional parkland, and no playing fields whatsoever. Even if one treats cobblestone plazas as parks (as one should), Venice's occasional courtyard opening falls far short of making it a park-rich town. Conversely, Buffalo, New York, has an interconnected park-and-parkway system that is ranked among the best of the iconic creations of Frederick Law Olmsted. There was a time when Buffalo was one of America's "Queen Cities," with more millionaires per capita than anywhere else. In fact, along with the Erie Canal, the park system was likely a part of its economic success. But today it is a struggling place with high poverty, low property values, and a population less than half of what it was in 1950. Buffalo's park system was the envy of American mayors in the 1880s, but it wasn't strong enough to overcome the city's decline. Today Buffalo consists of a wonderful and historic park system without much of a city to surround it.

The other challenge to figuring out the "correct" number of acres is the wide range of densities and forms of cities and the many different ways that Americans live on the land. From crowded New York to sparse Albuquerque or Oklahoma City, population density affects everything from transportation to retail to education to health to politics (see table 1.2 and appendix 1). It certainly affects the way people use parks. High-density living provides the opportunity for frequent positive human interaction, both planned and unplanned. It also, of course, provides the potential for conflicts around noise, privacy, smells, and demand for facilities.

Is it realistic to expect that dense cities—those that have, say, ten persons per acre (6,400 persons per square mile) or more—will be able to pack in as much parkland as lower-density cities, not to mention suburbs and rural areas? What about cities like Atlanta and Pittsburgh, which may not be extremely crowded with residents but experience a large influx of commuters every morning (see table 1.3)?

Or is the very concept of parkland and density a contradiction in terms? Let's consider the reverse: Is it realistic to expect that lower-density cities or suburbs will be able to pack in as much diversity of culture, retail, culinary opportunity, entertainment, and architecture as dense cities? Can every community provide a comparable level of service in every commodity to every resident? Parks make cities better,

Table 1.2 Howdy, Neighbor!
Population Density, Selected Cities

City	Area (Acres)	Population	Population Density (persons per acre)
New York	195,072	8,310,212	42.6
San Francisco	29,884	764,976	25.6
Chicago	145,362	2,836,658	19.5
Miami	22,830	424,662	18.6
Los Angeles	300,201	3,834,340	12.8
Detroit	88,810	916,952	10.3
Las Vegas	72,514	558,880	7.7
Dallas	219,223	1,266,372	5.8
Memphis	178,761	674,028	3.8
Kansas City, Mo.	200,664	475,830	2.4
Oklahoma City	388,463	547,274	1.4
Anchorage	1,258,880	279,671	0.2

Note: For full list, see appendix 1.
Source: Center for City Park Excellence, The Trust for Public Land

Table 1.3 Parks for Daytimers, Too?
Change in City Population Due to Commuters, Selected Cities

City	Resident Population	Estimated Daytime Population	Percentage Change in Daytime Population Due to Commuting
Washington, D.C.	572,059	982,853	71.8
Atlanta	416,474	676,431	62.4
Tampa	303,447	447,498	47.5
Pittsburgh	334,563	472,754	41.3
Chicago	2,896,016	3,038,344	4.9
Los Angeles	3,694,820	3,822,697	3.5
San Jose, Calif.	894,943	844,874	−5.6
Mesa, Ariz.	396,375	357,056	−9.9
Virginia Beach, Va.	425,257	376,226	−11.5
Arlington, Tex.	332,969	291,419	−12.5

Source: Census 2000, PHC-T-40

but at a certain point too much parkland means too little city. Perhaps one reason for the greatness of Central Park and Prospect Park is that Manhattan and Brooklyn are so short of parkland—less than 2 acres for every 1,000 residents in each borough. Like caviar, pearls, and true love, rarity makes it poignant. For this reason, it is much more instructive to compare the amount of park acreage in cities of the same approximate density type—comparing, say, Oakland with Seattle, or Phoenix with San Antonio, but not crowded Philadelphia with spread-out Tulsa (see table 1.4 and appendix 2).

Table 1.4 Parkland for People
Acres per 1,000 Persons, by Density Levels, Selected Cites

City	Population	Park Acres	Acres per 1,000
High-Density Cities			
Washington, D.C.	588,292	7,617	12.9
Philadelphia	1,449,634	10,886	7.5
Los Angeles	3,834,340	23,761	6.2
New York	8,310,212	38,229	4.6
Miami	424,662	955	2.2
Intermediate High-Density Cities			
St. Paul, Minn.	277,251	5,476	19.8
Oakland	401,489	5,217	13.0
Seattle	594,210	5,476	9.2
Cleveland	438,042	3,127	7.1
Anaheim, Calif.	333,249	864	2.6
Intermediate Low Density Cities			
San Diego	1,266,731	45,492	35.9
Phoenix	1,552,259	41,980	27.0
San Antonio	1,328,984	27,922	21.0
Atlanta	519,145	3,846	7.4
Mesa, Ariz.	452,933	2,619	5.8
Low-Density Cities			
Albuquerque	518,271	34,630	66.8
Jacksonville	805,605	46,241	57.4
Austin	743,074	26,271	35.4
Tulsa	384,037	7,336	19.1
Tucson	525,529	3,658	7.0

Note: For full listing, see appendix 2
Source: Center for City Park Excellence, The Trust for Public Land

CHAPTER 2

The Different Kinds of Parks and Their Uses

Figuring out the proper balance between parkland, structures, and streets on the urban canvas is an art more than a science. Figuring out how to accomplish this art in a public arena requires, first of all, a clearer understanding of what parkland is. Many different spaces and places are grouped under the nomenclature of "park": ballfields, woods, meadows, gardens, overlooks, playgrounds, lakes and lakeshores, seashores, riversides, wetlands, picnic areas, memorial grounds, historic sites, trails, greenways, parkways, boulevards, commons, plazas, squares, quadrangles, and courtyards, among others.

Notice that Gertrude Stein, after speaking of roses, did not say, "A park is a park is a park." Nor did Ronald Reagan, after speaking of redwoods, say, "If you've seen one park, you've seen them all."

The large number of park types, ranging from insect-filled wetlands that have no human visitors to center-city brick plazas that have no grass and sometimes even no trees, can be confounding to any planning process and even to a conversation. The vast number of activities that can and do take place in parks makes the discussion even more complex (see box 2.1).

Traditionally, park uses have been divided into two classes: "active" and "passive." This unfortunate nomenclature has caused countless hours of confusion and wasted analysis. There is no official definition of these words, and, in fact, they're often used as a kind of code by those who want to save green space but at the same time hope to prevent the kind of park creation that could bring in noisy outsiders. At the extremes the presumption is easy: "Active" is something like rugby while "passive" is something like sitting under a tree. But there is no clear dividing line between the two—no definition, just a feeling in the gut of the beholder. Try coming down the active scale: rugby, basketball,

Box 2.1

What People Do in City Parks: A Partial List

Traditional Team Sports
Play tennis, golf, basketball, football, hockey, baseball/softball, volleyball, cricket, rugby, soccer, lacrosse

Less Traditional Sports
Bike on trail, bike on road, skateboard, in-line skate, ice-skate, run on park road, run on trail, fish, throw a Frisbee, throw a ball, Frisbee golf, kickball, Hacky Sack, rock climb, ice climb, wall climb, swim, raft, kayak, canoe, row (crew), surf, windsurf, sail, throw horseshoes, lawn bowl/bocce, play shuffleboard, ski cross-country, ski downhill, archery, lift weights, do exercises

More-Active Non-Sports
Fly a model airplane, float model boats, run model cars, play tag, chase, play hide-and-seek, use playground equipment, use a swing set, dig in the dirt, play in the water, walk/hike, walk a pet, perform (e.g., mime, music), climb a tree, bungee jump, geo cache, orienteering, paddleboat, tai chi, have a race, fly a kite, use a hula hoop, ride a horse, scuba dive, snorkel, camp out, falconry

Less-Active Non-Sports
Eat, drink, picnic, orate, gather with friends or family, read, write, think, sing, garden, do yoga, meditate, watch wildlife, photograph wildlife, photograph people, paint, sketch, drive a car, sit in a parked car, drive a motorcycle, visit a nature center, build a sand castle, search for lost coins/jewelry, sunbathe

Other (Generally Considered Positive)
Take a nap, pick up litter, sell or buy arts and crafts, sell or buy food, stage a concert or play, have a party, talk on the phone, surf the Internet, send and receive e-mail, watch people, kiss, improvise games, hold a class, take part in an interpretive talk, watch a historical reenactment, perform community service, restore a landscape, restore a structure, take risks, carry out a search-and-rescue drill

Other (Generally Considered Negative)
Have sex, sell or buy drugs, use illegal drugs, fight, panhandle, draw graffiti, destroy property, hide

tennis, golf, lawn-bowling. Try going up the passive scale: sitting, strolling, walking, power-walking, jogging, running. The two concepts pass each other, at least in terms of calories expended, without ever hitting a boundary. And what about bicycling? Cycling has many of the attributes of so-called passive recreation since it is trail-based and can be performed so casually as to barely raise the heart rate; yet, in other circumstances, the obvious evidence of sweat and heavy breathing (not to mention pedestrians sometimes scattered in the wake) makes it undeniably "active."

Why even bother to classify activities? Because of that fuzzy word "park." If one person is seeking a quiet outdoor spot to read and another wants a place for her son to do tricks on his skateboard, they need a more descriptive word than "park" to communicate with each other. To make a comparison with transportation terminology, the word "road" is generalized, but it has a range of well-understood subcategories from "path" through "lane" and "street" and "avenue" to "interstate." Unfortunately, when it comes to parks, "passive" and "active" don't do the trick. Some people have suggested substituting more accurate words like "competitive" and "noncompetitive," where the former tends to require some kind of playing field, generally open, mowed or paved, rather flat, rather large, and often fenced to keep in a ball; while the latter generally has no requirements other than places to sit or walk. Others have suggested the words "regulated" and "unregulated." Here's the reality: "Competitive" or "regulated" activities tend to involve greater speed and violence, thus posing a threat to babies, children, seniors, women, men, pets, sunbathers, picnickers, and others, thus necessitating boundaries if not fences. "Noncompetitive" or "unregulated" is everything else. Admittedly, tossing a Frisbee or roller-skating on a plaza does pose a small risk to other park users, but the fact that it takes place in a noncompetitive fashion allows the activity to stop if a toddler ambles past or a senior rolls by in a wheelchair. (This is why bicycling is so hard to classify and why trails are often laden with conflicts. The spectrum from very casual family pedaling all the way up to competitive racing is huge. Communities that are most advanced in trail construction, like Minneapolis, have taken to installing two parallel treadways for users of different speeds and capabilities.)

Is all this an irrelevant, complex, and senseless exercise, akin to counting the number of angels that can fit on the head of a pin? Not really.

The park experience is intensely personal and can never be entirely quantified, but the size and composition of a park system certainly matters. As urban parkland gains in public attention and interest, many institutions from park departments to tourism agencies to travel magazines seek to put it into an understandable context. At first blush, sheer acreage seems to be the answer everyone is looking for (see appendixes 2 and 3), but it quickly becomes obvious that the issue has much more nuance.

Cities need space for both noncompetitive and competitive recreation. Competitive play is relatively straightforward since most sports have fields or courts with official shapes and sizes. But noncompetitive recreation varies widely—from people-oriented activities like watching and talking in plazas, meadows, lakeshores, playgrounds, dog parks, and on benches to nature-oriented activities like walking in forests, wetlands, deserts, and grasslands.

This is where some exciting new thinking is coming out of Portland, Oregon. Modifying earlier work done in rural areas by the U.S. Forest Service, planners in Portland analyzed every one of their city parks to determine the activities each one supports. Then, using a spectrum that ranges from spaces of extreme sociability to spaces of extreme ecological purity, they created a three-way classification they call "people-to-people" places, "people-to-nature" places, and "nature-to-nature" places. The former two represent different types of human recreation, the latter refers to pure conservation (or "green infrastructure"). The system is based on the relationship among experiences, settings, and activities, with experiences being paramount. The setting may be a spray ground and the activity may be getting wet with an eight-year-old friend, but it is the experience that will resonate for hours, days, maybe even months: sensory stimulation, camaraderie, feeling good, and adding something to the collective memory bank. Or the experience of a walk through quiet woods: psychic renewal, awe, a sense of connectedness with nature. A game of soccer? Exhilaration, teamwork, and muscular and intellectual skill. "People seek and remember recreation experiences," explained Sue Donaldson, former senior planner at the Portland Park and Recreation Department. "They may talk about a particular setting or an activity, but they usually mean they are seeking or have found an experience."

Instead of trying to squeeze multiple meanings into the single word "passive," the Portland system is truly three-dimensional. Adopting this system seems superior because it is so much more specific. It helps a city understand where it is strong and weak, where it has needs, and where it should spend money. "People-to-people" locations include such facilities as plazas, most squares and public space in traffic circles, skateboard parks, dog parks, playgrounds, basketball courts, tennis courts, and, in fact, all sports fields. "Nature-to-nature" includes all areas where natural processes are essentially unhindered by the activities of humans—forests, swamps, deserts, and the like. "People-to-nature" is perhaps the largest and most subtle category, picking up such diverse locations as greenways and trails, forests that have pathways through them, flower gardens, community gardens, meadows used for picnicking and sunbathing, ponds and lakes, and much more. (In theory a basketball court in a lush park could be termed a "people-to-nature" spot, but the Portland planners decided to treat all competitive sports—even golf, with its notably horticultural setting—as "people-to-people." "No matter how beautiful the setting," said Donaldson, "the real reason people come is to play against each other.") Clearly, toting up the actual land acreage by category in a real city is not easy, but doing so provides truly useful information. This system also helps agencies with budgeting and cost accounting; it's helpful to recognize, for instance, that "people-to-people" spaces are the most expensive to create and maintain, and "nature-to-nature" the least.

Is It Acres, Facilities, or Distance?

Before assessing how much parkland a city "should have," we need to consider facilities. For many years, researchers in the recreation field have analyzed Americans' desires for everything from baseball diamonds, football fields, and basketball courts to swimming pools and playgrounds. Although tastes change over time (racquetball boomed for a while and is currently in a decline, while kickball is rebounding from beyond corny to cutthroat cool), counting needs is a sound methodology. However, it has foundered in two different ways. First, competitive sports prove considerably easier to analyze than noncompetitive activities like walking and bench-sitting. Second, the discussion has often gotten bogged down with the debate over "neighborhood park" versus "community park" versus "district park" versus "regional park." What, if anything, is the relationship between a park's size, its type, and the facilities it contains?

There are few conversations as bizarre as those between planners and citizens when it's announced that "our city is over the standard for community parks but desperately short of neighborhood parks." Or "flush with district parks" but "critically in need of one more regional park." Yes, there is a germ of a rational idea there, but what can anyone do with this information? It might make sense to the developer of an enormous new housing project on the desert edge of El Paso, but where does it lead in the reality of present-day Boston or Los Angeles? Sometime back in the 1970s, it seems, creative flexibility was replaced by mechanistic guidelines: A neighborhood park, in one book of standards, was defined as being "centrally located within its one-quarter-to-one-half-mile service area, with well-drained soils and level topography and a recommended minimum size of 5 acres. It would have play structures, court games, informal playing open space, tennis courts, volleyball courts, shuffleboard courts, a horseshoe area, ice skating area, wading pool, and activity room, plus seven to ten off-street parking spaces." A community park was "between 20 and 50 acres with a higher-quality natural resource base, pulling from two or more neighborhoods with a service area of between a half-mile and three miles, and be easily accessed by way of arterial and collector streets." It would have "large play structures and/or (choose among) creative play attractions, game courts, informal ballfields for youth play, tennis courts, volleyball courts, shuffleboard courts, horseshoe areas, ice skating areas, swimming pools, swimming beaches, archery ranges, and golf areas, along with picnic and sitting areas, general open space, and ornamental gardens."

Instead of recognizing a shortage of, say, tennis courts or running trails, the conversation shifted to the need for a specific kind of park—which was usually too large or too expensive or too controversial to shoehorn into an existing neighborhood. It's not the acreage or park type *standard* that should motivate cities but the direct awareness of the *need*: the specific need for a dog park, or a skateboard bowl, or a place for picnicking, or woods to walk through. And those needs should come from the specific citizenry involved, not some idealized citizenry defined by a university guideline or trade association standard.

The other challenge to the "how much" question comes from the noncompetitive side of the spectrum—all those activities that don't have rules and official court dimensions. For, say, a soccer league, it's possible to determine how many teams there are, figure out how many games will be generated per day, and then calculate how many fields are needed. Of course, the size of the playing field is also known. In contrast, it is much tougher to determine the proper supply of such features as walking paths, benches, bike trails, picnic places, fishing spots, or, harder still, just plain woods, swampland, or desert—trailless "nature-to-nature" places. The ideal number of park benches or miles of pathway for every 1,000 urban residents is confounded by the issue of personal preference. If a walking trail through the woods contains one couple every 300 feet, is it pleasantly animated or overcrowded? How about one couple every 100 or every 50 feet? What about groups of a half-dozen teenagers each? If the amount of trail space is so minimal that you regularly bump into someone you know, is that fun or is it tedious? Alternatively, if the forest has one person every four acres, does the wild solitude feel blissful or scary? The right number of benches per bottoms may depend on etiquette. Is it acceptable to sit on a bench that is already occupied by another person? Or must those three unused spaces be left unfilled, even if all the other benches are taken? With a regulation sport like basketball, it's agreed that a 4,700-square-foot court will serve ten players (or, in high-density situations, twenty players, each group using one hoop). But with unregulated activities, it's more a matter of personal space, personal preference, and the conventions of the local community.

Again, instead of seeking or setting an official standard for, say, picnic-spots-per-1000-persons, it's more efficacious to set a standard for *how to devise a process* for meeting the need for picnicking, walking, bench-sitting, bird-watching, cycling, kite-flying, and more in *each specific community.*

Then there is the question of distance. Houston and Albuquerque, among other cities, have abundant total acreages of land yet have numerous neighborhoods that are almost devoid of parks. Los Angeles, while ranking 11th among big cities with more than 23,000 acres of parkland, has the majority of its park acres located in the mountainous and relatively inaccessible central section of the city. Meanwhile, many square miles of poorer neighborhoods lack any significant parks at all. Realistically, large segments of LA's 3.8 million residents are too far from a park to use one easily, conveniently, or frequently.

How should distance be measured, and how close should a park be? Unquestionably, the proper way to measure distance is physically, not chronologically. Miles, yards, feet, or meters—not minutes. Measuring by time serves only to add confusion. If a park is "ten minutes away," is that time measured in a car, on a bike, by power walking, or by strolling? In the ten minutes that a mother and toddler might travel three blocks, an auto on a freeway could go seven or eight miles. Perhaps the clearest statement for those who don't have a sense of distance is: "A quarter of a mile, or about five to six minutes of average walking." Also, measurement in generic "blocks" is ambiguous since the size of a block can vary dramatically; any use of "block" should be defined in feet.

Studies show that residents are more likely to use a park if it is close by, but in fact this is a subtle and complicated issue that gets to the heart of the many different ways people live in their environment. When planners draw concentric circles around parks, those zones are in fact averages and approximations of numerous personal decision-point factors that include physical strength, time, fear, traffic, companion-ship, and others (see box 3.1). Most cities don't have a proximity stan-dard, let alone an accounting of actual distances, but some have gone so far as to articulate an ambition (see table 3.1).

Many spread-out cities are settling for a goal of a park within a mile of every resident, which realistically is "car distance" for most people: doing the trek by foot, round trip, would take about 40 minutes, not counting any time in the park. Chicago is aiming for half a mile. (New York Mayor Michael Bloomberg called for a "ten-minute walk" but did not define that in feet.) Seattle and Long Beach differentiate between high-density and low-density neighborhoods and mandate closer spac-ing in more crowded areas. Denver took a practical approach: planners organized focus groups of primarily non-English speakers who were less likely to have cars. They heard clearly that those parents weren't comfortable with their unaccompanied children being more than six blocks away, so they chose that as a goal. (However, they didn't define the length of a Denver block.)

Table 3.1 A Park Too Far?
Goal for Maximum Resident Distance from a Park, Selected Cities

Agency	Maximum Distance Goal (in feet)
Miami	1,320
St. Paul, Minn.	1,320
San Jose, Calif.	1,760
Colorado Springs	2,640
Phoenix	2,640
St. Petersburg, Fla.	2,640
Bakersfield, Calif.	3,960
Tucson	3,960
Austin	5,280
Indianapolis	5,280
Wichita	5,280
Atlanta	10,560

Source: Center for City Park Excellence, The Trust for Public Land

Box 3.1

How Far to a Park Fourteen Scenarios

Scenario 1
You are a fourteen-year-old on the phone with some of your neighborhood friends. For play you have a choice between real basketball down the street and computer basketball in your room. Your mom doesn't have time to drive you, so you'd have to walk both ways. You feel like going out but you have a fair amount of homework. If the park is a quarter-mile away, you'd do it. If it's half a mile or farther, the walk is too time-consuming and a hassle—it's so much easier to just turn on the computer.

Scenario 2
You're a businesswoman working in center city. The weather is heavenly. An attractive downtown park nearby is a fun place to have lunch. You call your girlfriend. She says she needs to quickly buy a yogurt and also has to be back for a 1 o'clock meeting. If the park is one-tenth of a mile away, you've got time; any farther, forget it—you'll each just eat at your desk.

Scenario 3
You are twenty-five and love tennis. It's a pleasant Saturday and your schedule is open. The courts will be crowded. You have a car, so you really don't care how far you have to go—you'll pick up your partner and just drive around until you find a court that's available, even if you have to go clear across town.

Scenario 4
You are a pregnant mom with a two-year-old. You have a car but live in a crowded neighborhood where parking is a hassle, plus getting the toddler in and out of the car seat is a struggle. That points to walking, though walking gets harder for you every day. You have fifty minutes before naptime. If the playground is one-twentieth of a mile away you'll go; any farther and it's not worth it.

continued

Box 3.1 continued

Scenario 5
You try to run for forty-five minutes every morning before going to work. At your pace that means about four miles. There's a beautiful greenway in town, but getting to it means first traversing an unattractive neighborhood. If the greenway is a mile from your house, you do it and it's the best part of your day. If two miles, it's not worth it—you'd have to suffer through the ugly part and then turn around the moment you get to the park.

Scenario 6
You're seventy-eight years old, you live alone, and you don't drive any more. It hurts to walk but you like getting outside. If there is a park with benches within a tenth of a mile, it's a great place to sit and talk with friends. Any farther is too far, unless it's next to the market: you can take the bus a mile, buy your things, sit in the park a while, and then take the bus back home.

Scenario 7
You love to garden but live in an apartment. You'd be willing to rent a plot in a community garden up to a quarter-mile away, although realistically that half-mile round-trip walk gets tedious pretty fast. An eighth of a mile would be a lot better. It's a hard choice—you prefer the city, but if there's not a garden close by, you might just throw in the towel and move to a townhouse in the suburbs.

Scenario 8
You live in an apartment with your wife and three children, ages twelve, eleven, and nine. Plus, two twenty-something cousins are staying with you while they look for work and a place to live. Your place is cramped and noisy. You want the kids to play outside. You're comfortable with them being on the sidewalk out front, but for them that's boring. If there were a park directly across the street, it would be fine to send them over there—with the windows open, they'd only be a shout away. If the park were 100 yards away, well, maybe that would be okay if the oldest promised to be vigilant. Any farther, no—too risky.

Scenario 9

You're a stay-at-home dad with a four-year-old and a seven-year-old. Your city has a 500-acre park that is a wonderland of trails, meadows, woods, ponds, playgrounds and more. There is no parking in the park, and finding a space in the surrounding neighborhood is far from guaranteed. If you live in an apartment facing the park, you take the girls there almost daily; if you're half a mile away, you go once or twice a week; a mile, and it's more like monthly.

Scenario 10

You're a sixty-year-old widow living in an apartment with a golden retriever. The dog needs to go out three times a day. The outing can be a short jaunt to do his business, or it can be a longer exercising stroll that you prefer if you have the time. Both of you enjoy the dog park. If it's a quarter-mile or closer, you'd go almost daily. If it's half a mile, maybe only weekly: while the canine park is a treat, walking the dog on the sidewalk is a perfectly adequate substitute.

Scenario 11

You live in a townhouse directly across the street from a one acre park. The park contains a small grassy hill, a few trees, a playground, two chessboards, a basketball court, and a sculpture. The grass is rather threadbare, the concrete tables are chipped, one tree has graffiti on its bark, and the basketball court has a couple of root buckles. The park users today aren't overtly scary but they aren't inviting, either. (Of eleven, only three are female.) It's a beautiful morning. Your friend calls to suggest a picnic brunch in the park. You think for a long moment and say, "Why don't we walk over to Central Avenue and go to Starbucks?"

Scenario 12

You're fifty-two years old. When you undress, you wife says, "What is that spare tire around your middle?" Joining a gym would cost $80 a month, not insignificant for you. Buying the equipment would be even more. If there were a park with an exercise course closer than half a mile away, you'd rustle up a buddy, run over, and whip yourself into shape. If the park were farther than half a mile, you'd only do it if you could easily drive and park—running would take too long. If there were no parking, it's $960 a year for a gym.

continued

Box 3.1 continued

Scenario 13

You are thirteen. Your nearest park is half a mile away. Too far to walk, but an easy bike ride. You ask your mom if it's okay for you and a friend to do it. She gets that look on her face. You describe a back route that involves all lightly used streets except for the miserable crossing of Broadway and Washington. She thinks long and hard, then says no—maybe next year. You go out in the backyard and play with some old firecrackers you found.

Scenario 14

You are asked to coach a preteen girls' soccer team. Most of the girls are from your neighborhood, and practices start at 5:30 p.m. If there's a field near home, you'll enthusiastically volunteer. If the city assigns you a field in Riverside Park, three miles away, you'd have to drive straight from work and your wife would have to bring your daughter separately in the other car, stopping at McDonald's on the way. Realistically it wouldn't be worth the hassle, although you do desperately want her to get into Yale.

CHAPTER 4

Parks and Their Competition

There is a rarely discussed issue about parks, namely, what their competition is. Where else can citizens spend their time? People may "need" parks but they have also found many alternative ways of satisfying those needs. City parks face rivalry from home entertainment systems, gyms, restaurants, sidewalks, and backyards. Because of this, parks must be very good—better than the opposition. Ideally parks will be close and accessible. But if they are good enough, people are willing to travel farther and make more time available to use them. If it's difficult to increase the number of parks, another avenue is to stimulate the usage of the existing ones; even in crowded cities, many parks are underutilized.

The two ironclad requirements for a park to be well-used are safety and cleanliness. Beyond that, people are attracted to inspiring horticulture (trees, bushes, lawns, plantings) and impressive hardscape (pathways, walls, fences, benches, architecture). With money and care, these features can be sometimes raised to extraordinary heights (breathtaking flower gardens, stirring allées of mature trees, exquisite stonework, memorable fixtures). Sculpture, artwork, water elements, performance spaces, and views can double and triple the impact. All these help make parks competitive, help make them special places to return to and also to take out-of-town visitors. But parks can also compete with the more "regular" factors in our day-to-day world. These factors include food, exercise, entertainment, and intimacy.

Adding a food component to a park gives a jolt of energy, whether it's something minimal, like a movable cart vendor, or fancy, like a white-tablecloth restaurant. From San Diego's Balboa Park to Boston's Post Office Square, many parks already have facilities like these; many more could benefit from them. Alternatively (and maybe even better) are food opportunities on private property directly facing a park. This keeps the commercial and maintenance burden across the street while allowing the social benefits to inure to the park itself. A market that specializes in picnic food, a carry-out, a fast-food joint, a deli, a regular restaurant, a European-type outdoor café—any and all have marvelous synergies with a park, even if creating them might entail changing the zoning on one or more facing streets. With one colossal exception, this symbiosis is rare in the United States today. There are smidgeons of park-facing, food-purchasing opportunities across from the Boston Common, Dupont Circle in Washington, D.C., MacArthur Park in Los Angeles, Oakland Cemetery in Atlanta, and others, but they are nothing compared with rows of large, lively, umbrella-festooned outdoor restaurants facing parks in Paris, Madrid, Vienna, Berlin, Buenos Aires, and dozens of other European and South American cities. The one U.S. exception is the Riverwalk—Paseo del Rio—in San Antonio. The Riverwalk is made up of three miles of verdant trailway operated and maintained by the San Antonio Department of Parks and Recreation and serves as the green artery of a twenty-two-restaurant and twelve-hotel commercial enterprise that is the envy of every mayor in the country. More than 5 million tourists come to San Antonio annually, and virtually every one of them samples Paseo del Rio. Some park purists consider the Riverwalk too raucous (although there are many quiet segments), but it undeniably sets the standard for synergy between food, nature, and fun.

Providing opportunities for exercise is an important competitive niche for parks, which immediately brings to mind the challenge from private-sector gyms. For a certain key rich-and-radiant demographic and age group there is no question that private gyms cut into public park use. While these folks are but a small percentage of Americans, they are disproportionately urban and influential. However, there's no reason parks can't compete with gyms. In fact, while parks can't match the high-tech chrome-and-glass image, they have other strengths that private gyms cannot equal.

The simplest park exercise facilities consist of nonmovable wooden platforms with iron bars, often called "parcourses" (even though the original Parcourse Company has gone out of business). When first created, the parcourse concept got a lot of buzz, but many Americans found that traditional laborious exercises like pull-ups, push-ups, and sit-ups are too reminiscent of grade school physical education class. Many old parcourses remain in parks but few are heavily used. Today, more contemporary movable lever-based or spring-based machines seem to fare better. In Los Angeles in 2007, County Supervisor Gloria Molina teamed up with Kaiser Permanente and the Trust for Public Land to fund the installation of "Fitness Zones" in five parks in neighborhoods whose residents are disproportionately overweight and unhealthy. Using no electricity and built to be durable enough for the outdoors, the equipment runs on what its manufacturer, TriActive America, calls "exercise power." The experiment was so successful that dozens more communities asked for them.

If positioned and marketed properly, fitness equipment can have three powerful competitive advantages over private gyms. First, cost: It is free to use. Second, the exercise area can be located within or directly adjoining a children's playground (or an off-leash dog park) so that the parent, grandparent, caregiver, or pet owner can do something physically beneficial while the child or animal plays. (The president of TriActive reports that children who get bored on the playground often join their moms or nannies on one of the fitness machines; however, there doesn't yet seem to be a workable fitness machine for a dog.) Third, Fitness Zones, unlike gyms, are television-free areas and do not promote individualization; if they are laid out so that the equipment is clumped into twos and threes, they can become powerful communication spaces for strengthening friendships and for building community social capital (also known as "gossiping").

Then again, instead of competing, parks and private gyms may be able to collaborate. Cities can encourage—or zone—private gyms so as to be located directly across from a park, increasing the conjunction of healthy people and healthy places. How nice it would be to ascend to a gym's second floor and stair-step while looking out over a beautiful park, and to then eat a picnic meal there afterward. Or, if the gym is located alongside a linear park trail, it could perhaps offer a rebate each time a member comes by bike instead of by car (and then convert half its parking lot into a garden).

Clearly the rise of fabulous electronic gadgetry poses a severe challenge to the importance, centrality, and need for parks. Regimented electrons have allowed the privatization of all kinds of activities that formerly had to be public. First, it was merely converting park band concerts to records or radio; then came portraying park sports on television. Then came rudimentary games to be played with a joystick. Both were so much fun and so convenient that they severely cut into the time available for park activities. Now the physical games themselves are starting to migrate to the television. In the past, if one wanted to play tennis and did not belong to a private club, one played in the park. That's what young Arthur Ashe did in Richmond, Virginia; Billie Jean King did in Long Beach; and the Williams sisters did in Compton, California. Today there is a sensational and seductive electronic technology that enables a player to stand in front of a TV and swing a remote control like a racket. (The virtual feeling is so engaging that there have been numerous real injuries to players and bystanders.) Sports and entertainment have merged, but not to the benefit of parks.

It may not be feasible to install video game or television arcades in parks, but there are numerous ways that parks can fight back on the entertainment front. In fact, parks are the *original* when it comes to entertainment. Live music of all sorts, with or without a fee, gives a park an edge over almost any other venue, especially the average home. Theater, dance, art exhibits, craft-making, and even nighttime movies and sunrise exercises can all deliver the kind of buzz that makes a park a neighborhood's leading attraction rather than its pathetic backwater. The Chess House in Central Park has dozens of boards, indoors and out, in an unbeatable location to exchange rooks (or just to watch)—quite a different experience than on the tiny screen of a video console or cellular phone. In Austin, when the Austin Parks Foundation sponsored the movie *Napoleon Dynamite,* 1,200 people came out for a memorable evening in Republic Park. Washington, D.C.'s National Gallery Sculpture Garden, which is a formal, slightly stuffy space during normal hours, becomes absolutely *the* place to be on Friday evenings when there is live jazz—every square inch is covered by people picnicking on blankets, talking, and watching one another. There is now even a music technology for children's playgrounds—a company called SoundPlay creates giant thumb pianos, metallophones, marimbas, and pipe drums with large mallets and pentatonic scales for kids to play real songs together or just make harmonic noise.

Finally, there is intimacy. Most people's backyards aren't as nice as most parks, but people with yards nevertheless often tend to stay in them. The convenience, of course, is unbeatable but it's also because the yard is convivial and private. Parks will never be private—that's the whole point—but they can be designed so that they have some nooks and crannies that are a bit more genial. Utilizing curving walkways, groves or rows of trees, sophisticated plantings, whimsical structures, gazebos, and other landscape techniques can create room-like spaces that play off the open vistas of meadows and lakes. Even just doing a better job with seating areas can make a big difference. Sitting on a bench is fine for watching the world go by, but most couples—and certainly most foursomes and sixsomes—would rather be able to directly or partially face each other or sit in a square or circle. Face-to-face benches, face-to-face chairs, tables with seats, or, best of all, movable chairs make a park experience a lot more like what someone would arrange in her yard.

CHAPTER 5

Neighborhoods Are Not All Created Equal

Neighborhoods can be distinguished from one another by dozens of characteristics, some plain, some subtle. In the context of parks, several key considerations—the "Big Six"—rise to the top. They are population density, wealth, cars, bicycles, sidewalks, and time.

From every perspective, population density is the most important factor in ascertaining park need. For one thing, dense neighborhoods simply have more people in a given amount of space. There are fewer private yards. Even while the streets are generally narrower, more clogged, and less usable as "open space," residents have fewer cars, meaning it's harder for them to get to distant sports fields or escape to nature. Dense neighborhoods have taller buildings that block sunlight. The parks they do have are likely to be more crowded with users. Buffering the surrounding housing from noise and nighttime sports lighting is more difficult. While dense neighborhoods have many advantages, their livability suffers without a generous scattering of parks.

On the other hand, there is nothing that gives a park more visual "pop" than being surrounded by the walls of buildings. Similarly, the pleasant surprise of coming across a park in a crowded district is like a syncopated beat of stop-time silence in a driving jazz composition. Existing parks that were formerly hard to notice in low-rise areas become ever more palpable and valuable as they evolve into green "rooms" within a denser, redeveloping neighborhood. (It is ironic that parks simultaneously mitigate and undermine urban density; dogmatic urbanophiles have even been known to speak out against large parks: nothing about the interface between cities and parks is straightforward or simple.)

Analyzed objectively, wealthier neighborhoods have less need for nearby parks than poorer areas. The rich are likely to have bigger yards, grander trees, and more private amenities like barbeque grills and even pools and tennis courts. Or, if they live in apartment buildings, they may have the use of workout rooms, game courts, rooftop decks, and swimming pools. The wealthy own more second homes and have longer vacations during which to get out of town. A larger percentage of the wealthy belong to private clubs that provide swimming, golf, tennis, and other sports. Between backyards and the ability to eat out more often at restaurants, they have less need for picnic spots. Poorer people, on the other hand, need and seek the many collective benefits provided by publicly supported parks. This is evidenced by every analysis of voting patterns in park referenda around the nation—lower-income citizens vote most strongly for park funding measures.

Also, cars make a huge difference. A relationship between cars and parks may sound shocking, but low-density neighborhoods with high levels of car ownership and easy parking do not require as many parks nearby. Residents may *like* having parks but, as we've seen, cars greatly reduce the challenge of distance (at least for the age group that can drive), pulling distant parks into a realistic orbit of reachability. Also, by definition, a low-density neighborhood already has a considerable amount of generalized open space, even though most of it is not public and much of it may consist of ungreen parking areas. If a lot of nonspecialized parkland is inserted into low-density neighborhoods, it is guaranteed to be used very lightly or not at all. (This is not true of specialized parks, from soccer complexes to tennis centers to botanical gardens, which can generate large numbers of visitors by the nature of their regional draw.) In the inverse of the density paradox, the way to maximize the parkland efficiency of low-density areas is to radically increase the amount of housing and commercial development around the edges of parks—using parks to stimulate development.

Bicycles, in theory, greatly extend the reach of a park since in a given amount of time the average person can bike about four times farther than he or she can walk. In practice, bikes don't help all that much since cycling makes up such a tiny mode share of the transportation universe. It's not enough to have a park that is delightful to ride *in*, it must also be delightful, or at least feasible, to ride *to*, and that is still a barrier for most Americans. Best is the park that has an off-road greenway trail connection (or several) leading right to it, like Gas Works Park in Seattle, served by the Burke-Gilman Trail; Lake Calhoun in Minneapolis, served by the Midtown Greenway; or Rock Creek Park in Washington, D.C., served by the Capital Crescent Trail. Second best is the park well served by feeder roads with bike lanes, slow speeds, and other safety features. The principal age group that can really benefit from the opportunity for bike transportation consists of eleven- to seventeen-year-olds. (Among the other age groups, most people who don't walk are either able to drive or must be driven.) Unfortunately, the parents of these children are often afraid to let them bike on busy city streets. Thus, extremely park-poor neighborhoods could somewhat mitigate their disadvantage by demanding outstanding on-street bicycle facilities to extend the reach for some users. Also, bike use helps reduce the amount of park space wasted on automobile parking; bicycling can thus be nudged upward by the installation of parking meters to charge for auto parking in and around parks.

Neighborhoods with great sidewalks may not need quite as many parks. Sidewalks are not given much thought by park advocates, but good ones actually serve some of the same people-to-people sociability functions as parks and plazas. Many have steps or stoops to sit on and railings to lean against; a few even have official benches, with or without advertising. If they have great shade-producing trees, so much the better. In *The Death and Life of Great American Cities*, Jane Jacobs writes, "Lowly, unpurposeful and random as they may appear, sidewalk contacts are the small change from which a city's wealth of public life may grow." Of course, parks do many things that sidewalks can't, but sidewalks have the major advantages of being closer to home and of often feeling safer. Conversely, neighborhoods with a poor sidewalk environment or no sidewalks at all can get partial compensation through more parks. A sprinkling of pocket parks here and there, of course, will not serve to protect walkers from the mess of road grit, the annoyance of hodge-podge street parking, and the danger of auto traffic. But the parks can pick up a portion of the missing social contacts in sidewalk-less communities, particularly if the green areas are designed not as little cul-de-sac endpoints but rather as pass-throughs on the way to the store, the school bus stop, the cleaner, and the pharmacy.

An experience in Los Angeles in 2003 demonstrated the similarity between parks and sidewalks. In East Los Angeles, the low-income, historically immigrant Boyle Heights neighborhood is so short of parkland that exercise-hungry residents took to jogging around historic

Evergreen Cemetery, a private graveyard in their midst. But the sidewalk environment, with root bulges, deep potholes, and few safe crossing areas, was dangerous. Organizing into the Evergreen Jogging Path Coalition, neighbors successfully lobbied the city to appropriate $800,000 to encircle the cemetery with a 1.5-mile, top-of-the-line new rubberized sidewalk that has become the pride of the area. Since then, use has increased from 200 people per day to more than 1,000, including also walkers, dog-walkers, stroller-pushers, and socializers. Even though the cemetery doesn't function as a park, its sidewalk has almost become one.

And finally, there is time. Lack of time is a major barrier to park use. Many Americans, including children, are simply too busy to indulge in more than an occasional park experience. (One reason unemployed persons seem to be overrepresented on the benches of certain city parks is that they have the time.) The closer a park is, the more it allows a quick trip to be squeezed into a busy schedule. This, again, tends to militate toward greater need in lower-income communities. Although many upper-income people may feel their lives are filled to and over the brim, in fact it's an even harder struggle for those who must juggle more than one job, numerous chores, and multiple responsibilities, particularly in a one-parent situation without paid help. Conversely, neighborhoods with fewer busy people—more retirees, more stay-at-home moms—may be able to get by with somewhat fewer nearby parks. Less stressed people have a bit more time to get to a park, use it, and get back home again.

Many of these factors merely represent tendencies, not commandments; there are enough outliers and exceptions to defeat any attempt at hard-and-fast rules. However, rolling together all six considerations helps us bring into some focus who it is that most needs parks: *people who are more time constrained and who live in neighborhoods that are densely populated and less wealthy, with fewer cars and inadequate bike and pedestrian facilities.* Ironically, these kinds of communities do not normally have the muscle to get more parks through the political process, a topic that will be discussed shortly.

CHAPTER 6

It's Not How Much but Who and Why

The proper answer to "How much parkland should our city have?" is: "Who wants to know, and why?" Understanding motivations and political realities is more helpful than hoping to be rescued by standards. Since there is no feasible absolute numerical standard, the question is ultimately political. Political questions must be dealt with politically. Let's see why.

Of the people who hope to rely on a parkland standard, the majority fall into one of two camps: (1) those who are unhappy with the current situation and are advocating to change it and (2) those who are tasked with responding to that advocacy. Almost no one is interested in a standard purely as an intellectual exercise; those who care usually have one agenda or another. Moreover, of the dissatisfied challengers of the status quo, the vast majority believe their city needs more parkland. (There are only two groups who would seek a standard to justify *reducing* the amount of urban parkland: antitax dogmatists who want to pare government spending and the occasional developer who wants to build something on an existing park.) Instead of attempting to establish a simple standard that has been proved ineffective, let's take each possible actor and see if there isn't a better way of meeting his or her needs.

Potential actor number one is a nongovernmental organization that wants more parkland. It might be a single-issue group interested in baseball or soccer fields or bike trails or dog parks or wilderness, or it might be a citywide organization working to expand green space more comprehensively. Normally, this group would begin by approaching the mayor or city council with a straightforward request for more parkland. But if, as is often the case, the request is rebuffed, group members usually look for ammunition to bolster their cause. A standard is obvious and potent and certainly appears a much easier route than organizing a full-fledged citywide political campaign to accomplish the same goal. (Of course, the approach only works if the city's acreage is below the national standard.)

Assuming for a moment that there is a national standard and that the city doesn't measure up, who exactly is this ammunition to be used against? If the mayor and council are predisposed toward adding parkland—most likely because they've gotten feedback from their constituents—they will probably take steps in that direction even without needing to be told about a standard. If they are not so predisposed, they won't. We've all heard the responses of politicians who don't want to do something: "That standard was developed for places like Oregon—we're completely different from Oregon"; "That's for warm-weather cities—we're a three-season city"; "That's for places with cheap land—our land is too costly"; "That's for suburban places—we're much more densely populated"; "That's for cities where almost everyone is the same—we're among the most diverse communities in the country"; "That's for them, not for us."

If not to convince the mayor, perhaps the standard is helpful to rally the troops—regular folks who think there should be more parkland but may be timid about being seen as greedy. Folks who aren't sure if asking for more might look like overreaching. Folks who are reluctant to speak up before knowing how their city compares with a standard. Perhaps the standard can be used to build the base. But, again, is this the best way to move forward? For one thing, what if the city already exceeds the standard? Would this put an end to any and all further discussion—even if a park proposal were particularly appealing and justifiable? What if a city had the "wrong" kind of parkland—wetlands instead of ball fields, or golf courses instead of forests? What if the people of the city just happened to be more park-oriented (or less park-oriented) than the people of other cities? Is relying on a standard a better way to rally the troops than the more straightforward mechanism of saying, "We need more parkland" or "We *want* more parkland"?

Potential actor number two is the planning director. For legal and other reasons planners prefer to use standards to justify their actions. But preference is generally trumped by reality. It's well known that the average city planning department operates reflexively more often than proactively—it tends to *respond* to the ideas and desires of developers rather than steering the process. (Recognizing that fact, some city park departments don't even *have* planners of their own.) While a planning department may want more parkland in a city (or in a particular neighborhood), that's not likely to happen without the enthusiastic support of the surrounding community and/or of a developer. The developer is more likely to respond to an offer of increased density or some other transfer of value; the well-organized community's political muscle is likely to be more powerful than a simple numerical standard. Moreover, nearly any plan in a modern city involves at most a small subarea, a space so diminutive that it cannot on its own do much to rectify a shortage of parkland and meet a standard. Even a redevelopment as massive as the billion-plus-dollar conversion of the old Atlantic Steel site in Atlanta involved a total of only 138 acres, compared with the full 84,316 acres of Atlanta. By devoting 11 acres of that site to parkland, it increased Atlanta's citywide parkland percentage from 4.56 percent to 4.57 percent of total land area. Of course, everything helps, and after dozens of redevelopments that used a park standard, a city would move incrementally in the right direction. But it would probably move more quickly by using a transparent and democratic public process that unleashed the enthusiasm of park-oriented citizens.

Potential actor number three is the mayor or the city manager. Again, chances are she is much more interested in the politics of the situation than if there is or isn't a standard being met. If she is positively disposed to parks, the main task is assuaging or neutralizing the opposition. If she herself is against any more parkland, advocates probably have only two options: organizing a full-fledged political campaign to change her mind or becoming part of an election campaign to replace her with someone else.

Two cities in Florida provide an enlightening insight into the politics of urban parkland acquisition. Jacksonville, at 839 square miles the second most expansive city in the nation (after Anchorage, Alaska), has ample quantities of park and preserve land, as we have seen, far exceeding any standard ever set for acres per capita (see appendix 2). Miami, one of the smallest and most densely populated major cities in the country (with 425,000 people on only 36 square miles), is near the bottom when it comes to park acres per capita. Yet, in 1999 Jacksonville Mayor John Delaney launched an immense $300-million land acquisition campaign called "Preservation Project Jacksonville" that took the city even further over any conceivable standard and placed it near the very top of all large American citeis. Meanwhile, between 2000 and 2008 Miami actually lost parkland, turning a portion of one of its parks over to the police for a horse stable and making other waterfront park acreage available to two museums. The concept of standards neither held Jacksonville back from amassing even more nor propelled Miami forward from its shortage.

All these factors point in a different direction—a direction of setting a standard for *how to devise a process* for setting a parkland goal rather than providing the acreage number itself. Ultimately it is up to the culture of each city to determine its "correct" amount of parkland based on a complex and unique interplay of history, geography, geology, hydrology, climate, population density, commerce, age distribution, wealth, civic spirit, and perhaps most important, leadership. For innumerable reasons the results will come out differently from one city to the next; the critical factor, however, is that the process itself is inclusive, transparent, and fair.

CHAPTER 7

A Process Rather than a Standard

Is there a way that residents of a city can come to agreement on the amount of parkland and the number of facilities and programs they want? While there may not be a universal standard for the right amount of urban acreage, is there a standard for a *process* to figure it out?

Well, yes. It is called master planning, and, when done right, it's a powerful process to guide change. Master planning is how the whole community—from the least engaged citizen and even his child all the way through park professionals, academics, advocates, business leaders, and up to the city council and mayor—can have a robust, meaningful dialogue about the current and future status of parks and recreation in the city. (Master planning is also carried out for other urban systems such as transportation, water, health, and economic development; the separate plans are eventually rolled together into the comprehensive plan.) The most visible outcome of the procedure is the written master plan but in some ways day-to-day and month-to-month conversations during the process are more significant, at least in communities where planning is conducted seriously and respectfully. Master planning provides guidance for elected officials to appropriate funds, take action, and set deadlines for accomplishments.

Many communities create master plans. Fewer, however, are successful at implementing them, which is why many plans end up sitting on shelves. Ideally the master planning process will yield the number of park acres that each community wants, not an amount specified by an official number. Then, ideally, the political process will deliver on-the-ground results based on support for the master plan. Unfortunately, there is many a slip 'twixt cup and lip. Powerful players, whether elected, appointed, or self-appointed, can opaquely insert themselves in the process, skewing or short-circuiting it entirely. Many large cities today are demonstrably short of parkland, including the Arizona cities of

Table 7.1 How Green Is My City?
Parkland as a Percent of City Area, Selected Cities

City	Area (acres)	Park Acres	Percent
High-Density Cities			
New York	195,072	38,229	19.6%
Boston	30,992	5,040	16.3%
Los Angeles	300,201	23,761	7.9%
Miami	22,830	1,359	6.0%
Santa Ana	17,280	357	2.1%
Intermediate High-Density Cities			
Minneapolis	35,130	5,864	16.7%
Seattle	53,677	6,170	11.5%
Buffalo	26,240	2,140	8.2%
Cleveland	49,650	3,127	6.3%
Stockton	35,200	665	1.9%
Intermediate Low-Density Cities			
San Diego	207,575	45,492	21.9%
Raleigh	73,600	12,252	16.6%
Sacramento	62,180	5,811	9.3%
Mesa	79,990	2,619	3.3%
Fresno	66,791	1,507	2.3%
Low-Density Cities			
Albuquerque	115,608	34,630	30.0%
El Paso	159,405	27,289	17.1%
Virginia Beach	158,903	17,853	11.2%
Louisville	246,400	15,902	6.5%
Tucson	124,588	3,658	2.9%

Source: Center for City Park Excellence, The Trust for Public Land

Tucson and Mesa, and the California cities of Santa Ana, Fresno, Stockton, and Anaheim. (While official standards are not useful, straightforward comparisons most definitely are; see table 7.1 and appendix 3.) Being near the bottom of a list is not necessarily what these cities' residents want, nor is it in any plan. All probably have thick documents in archives showing wonderful swaths of parkland and numerous recreational facilities. But a great plan, unaccomplished, is still a failure. It is either deficient on its own merits or it was not carried out properly. There really should be no dividing line between the plan and its implementation. Ideally, the American Planning Association would never give an award for a mere plan; awards should be reserved for that rarer accomplishment—the great plan perfectly realized.

The exemplary master plan consists of ten components:

- An analysis of current conditions;
- A survey that measures the public's interests and its willingness to pay for improvements;
- A public outreach component;
- A cost analysis for any new improvements and programs;
- An analysis of potential income from facilities and programs;
- A ranking system for prioritizing the implementation of the elements of the plan;
- A decision-making process;
- A budget;
- A timeline for implementation; and
- An evaluation component (that ties in with the next current conditions report and starts the process over again).

We will go through each of these components in a bit of detail in the next two chapters.

CHAPTER 8

Stop, Look, and Listen

A master plan begins with a current conditions report. For parkland, that means not only the obvious—acres of parkland, number of playgrounds, miles of trails, size of workforce, estimated cost of needed capital repairs, and so on—but also more nuanced factors, with a deeper reach into the fabric of the city: something that is broad, informative, contextual, and educational to everyone from expert to general citizen. What is the park system's role in reducing stormwater runoff and ambient air pollution? How much property tax is added to the city's coffers by higher assessments due to proximity to outstanding parkland? How many users does the system get—not only registered softball players and yoga students but even those just walking through parks on the way to work? How much would residents have to pay in the private marketplace if they didn't have a free park system serving as their gym, their flower garden, their tennis or swimming club, their festival venue, their aviary, and a play-gym for their kids? How much is rush-hour car congestion being reduced by people cycling to work on park trails and greenways? How much is community cohesion increased through neighbors working together to clean up parks, pull out invasive vines and weeds, and plant flowers and trees? How much is citywide tourist revenue increased by park events and by the general attraction of beautiful parks? And finally, how does the park system compare to that of other pertinent places—the competitor cities upriver, downriver, across the state, and across the country? It's one thing for, say, Indianapolis to be below a theoretical standard in something, but to be below archrival Columbus, Ohio? Now, them's fighting numbers! Same with Tulsa and Oklahoma City, San Diego and Los Angeles, Dallas and Atlanta, Chicago and New York, and dozens of other friendly urban rivals. Rejecting hollow standards does not mean discounting the immense importance of data.

None of this data is easily accessible. Unlike such fields as transportation and retail, the park arena does not have a long tradition of data collection—or, perhaps more accurately, the earlier tradition of counting atrophied after World War II. While city transportation directors today can provide reams of facts about every conceivable past, present, and future movement of an automobile, city park directors are generally stymied by even such an obvious question as "How many people do you serve in a year?" In their defense, counting is not inexpensive and, with steady budget and staff reductions, collecting statistics was one of the operations lost in the cutbacks. Still, as we always say, "If you don't count, you don't count." The lack of information unquestionably contributed to the decline in the funding and importance of park systems. Fortunately, city park data collection seems to be back on the upswing, partly because of the national-level work of the Center for City Park Excellence, the Rails-to-Trails Conservancy, and the U.S. Forest Service and partly because of renewed interest by local organizations and institutions such as New Yorkers for Parks, the San Francisco Neighborhood Parks Council, Park Pride in Atlanta, the University of Pennsylvania, the University of Illinois, Texas A&M University, and others.

The next step for a master plan is to survey the public's interests and its willingness to pay. Again, these data are far superior to a theoretical standard. Different cities have different cultures, and these mores spill over into park use. Extreme sportiness? Think Seattle, Denver, and Minneapolis. (Denver and Minneapolis even had a friendly competition in the summer of 2008 over which could attain a higher level of bicycle use during the Democratic and Republican national conventions.) Beach and pool lounging? Maybe Los Angeles and Miami. Getting a bit dressed up and going for a park promenade? New York, Boston, and San Francisco. Skipping the parks entirely and sticking with private yards or private clubs? Perhaps Memphis, Houston, Tulsa, and Oklahoma City—these four cities had among the lowest per-capita park spending levels of all big cities in a recent year. Seattle, on the other hand, spent three times the median of all the cities, per resident, and Minneapolis spent almost twice the median. Spending is extremely revealing. Assuming that politicians pay attention to their constituents, and assuming that other things are equal, per-person spending will roughly correlate with a city's commitment to its parks (see appendix

4). Surveying for willingness-to-pay is a tried-and-true methodology for parks and conservation. For instance, in 2003, the East Bay Regional Park District, in Oakland, surveyed voters and found that 88 percent of them believed that regional parks and trails were a "valuable public resource"; 86 percent of them recognized the need to properly maintain the system; and 77 percent indicated a willingness to pay an extra assessment of $5 per year for that purpose. A measure for this amount was put on the ballot, and it passed.

The next element of master planning involves public outreach—truly interacting with the citizenry. This two-sided coin requires both educating and listening, telling the public what the park system consists of and what the department does, and also finding out what is on residents' minds. One city that is particularly outstanding in this realm is Portland, Oregon, which has an independently elected city auditor whose office does an extraordinary annual survey of resident satisfaction with every aspect of city government services and then rates the agencies' quality. Also, the park department's Web page has a special place inviting residents to propose community-initiated park improvements. Park Director Zari Santner, who is legendary for her attention to resident concerns, recounted one telling incident. "There was a private dairy that went out of business on a very small site. Though the city cleaned it up, we didn't want it—It was only a quarter of an acre. The local residents asked for it as a park. We agreed that the area was park-poor, but we just felt it was too small. Despite our skepticism, they were adamant, they raised money, and eventually got it deeded as parkland. They were very persistent and we were very hesitant, but we worked with them. Frankly, in retrospect, I think they were right."

Minneapolis, which, uniquely, has an elected park board and thus faces street-level, issue-oriented political campaigns about parks every two years, is also finely attuned to resident concerns. When planners noticed that most of their meeting audiences consisted of single-family homeowners, they instituted a special program to distribute upcoming event leaflets in multifamily buildings, apartment by apartment. Though an added cost, it was an effort to make up for inequities and provide more balance in park planning.

On the other hand, some park agencies seem to insulate themselves from, or even rebuff, their constituents. One reason for the massive overhaul of the once-inept Chicago park system in the 1990s was a series of sensational exposés in the Chicago *Daily News* revealing, among other things, that the majority of scheduled recreation programs never actually took place.

One way to spot potential shortcomings before they become front-page headlines is to check how the department is responding to up-and-coming trends. Park facility types and recreational pastimes evolve all the time, and each metamorphosis forces the agency into a budgetary and staffing balancing act. It gets tugged by a new constituency to make changes while it already has millions of dollars sunk in fixed costs, programs, and maintenance routines that would be easier not to modify.

Two hot recent passions are for off-leash dog parks and skateboard parks. Both are problematical because of noise, smell, user conflicts, liability, or because of real or perceived management challenges based on just plain newness. On the other hand, dog owners and skateboarders bring enthusiastic new coteries to urban parks at a time when some former constituencies—golfers and rollerbladers, for instance—are losing steam. Dog owners, in particular, are an extensive and growing group with considerable political clout and personal wealth who could potentially give a boost to park systems at election time, end-of-year donation time, and every day in between. By the end of 2007, Portland, Oregon, with a population barely exceeding half a million, responded to requests by creating thirty-one off-leash dog parks. At the same time, eleven major cities, including Jacksonville, Wichita, Detroit, Anaheim, Buffalo, Jersey City, and Tulsa, hadn't created a single one. Nineteen others, including populous places like Columbus, Louisville, Memphis, Baltimore, Washington, D.C., and Atlanta, had created only a single off-leash dog park each. The story for skate parks is similar. While fourteen major cities had not built a single skate park by the end of 2007, Las Vegas showed extraordinary responsiveness to citizen demand by constructing ten, Long Beach, California, opened eight, and Sacramento unveiled seven. The more carefully a city does outreach and then listens to the information that comes back, the more likely it is to respond nimbly and effectively. That's not a guarantee, but the converse is: A city that doesn't listen will never respond.

CHAPTER 9

Analyze and Prioritize

After actively listening, it's time to start analyzing. The next two elements of the master plan are economic—looking at costs and also at potential income. This is not "budgeting"—that comes later. This is merely becoming cognizant of how much things would cost and how much they might generate, so as to inform the decision-making process. This is the way to begin subjecting the fervor of a small subset of park users to the reality test of the population at large. In the absence of competition over resources, almost no one would speak out against any enthusiastic group—whether mountain bikers, disc golfers, beach volleyball players, or dog owners—who were pressing for more space or programs. After all, live and let live. But with dollars involved, the trade-offs come into focus. A top-of-the-line molded concrete skateboard park might cost as much as four more modest facilities that use aboveground, prefabricated metal forms. And those might cost twice as much as a pair of simple sand volleyball courts. A mountain bike course might be as inexpensive as clearing a path through an already-owned forest, or it might necessitate the pricey purchase of entirely new land to avoid antagonizing an existing birdwatching constituency. Conversely, depending on a city's history and its culture of service to residents, certain activities can be priced to generate income. For golf, league fields, and ice-skating on a rink there is usually a charge. Swimming, tennis, flower gardens, and festivals may or may not have a fee, depending on a city's philosophy. Trail use, pick-up games, playgrounds, and informal picnics are always free. Not that income—or, for that matter, cost—should be the controlling factor. Public parks have always been and should always be outside the traditional hand of the marketplace, but cost obviously adds an important dose of reality to any conversation.

Next, how do we rank the many disparate needs? How do we choose between additional flowers, better-pruned trees, a first-ever dance instructor, longer hours at pools, higher salaries, better lighting, a refurbished irrigation system, a volunteer coordinator, a Little League championship series, three new acres downtown, 150 new acres adjacent to the airport, and the thousands of other competing wants and opportunities? This is where transparency and opacity really matter. It doesn't do any good to have an open process for soliciting input if the process for making decisions is then secretive, biased, or preordained. Even under the best of circumstances, this is the point when lofty and beautiful platitudes sometimes descend to the gutter and formerly genteel policy contestants can end up looking like mud wrestlers. If the prioritization is done incorrectly, a community can lose faith in the process. Done right, this is where the training of excellent planners, the listening and analytical skills of capable facilitators, and the leadership skills of effective politicians all come together in a harmonious whole. It won't be perfect for anyone but it will be good for everyone.

Next comes making the actual recommendation, which means balancing equity and politics. Each fosters a different kind of trust. Responding to calls for equity fosters trust that government can do what's fair. Responding to the pressures of politics—politics in the best sense of the word, politics that demonstrates the passion felt by constituents—fosters trust that government can listen and hear. The public at large appreciates decisions based on objective comparative factors like acreage, spending, distance to a park, facility types, and facility age. Members of single-issue groups appreciate decisions based on expressed desire and conviction, whether it is soccer fields, dog parks, or wilderness. Leaning too far either way can result in residents' feeling of anger and alienation. In Miami, park advocates have been frustrated that most decisions are made politically, with little attention to objective data. In Washington, D.C., it's the opposite: Park advocates criticize the National Park Service for being so insulated from local politics that it operates "by the book," ignoring the needs and wants of citizens. While allowing too much entrepreneurial politics turns parks into thoughtless playthings of the rich and powerful, too little politics makes park systems moribund. Among other indicators, Washington, D.C., is so resistant to constituent politics that it still has not a single park restaurant and has only one dog park and one skatepark, neither of which are on National Park Service land.

After that ranking procedure, the final three steps are, if not easier, at least more cut and dried: developing a budget, developing a timeline, and designing an evaluation component.

CHAPTER 10

Don't Forget Money and Time

Budgeting, of course, is not simple. It requires good knowledge about the costs of materials, salaries for different kinds of work, contingencies, and also how long tasks take. But a budget is an absolute must: A master plan without one is like car without a key. Nothing will happen—nothing *can* happen—until a city council approves a budget and appropriates some money. Admittedly, creating a budget is scary. Sometimes the numbers for what detractors will call "just a park" can seem so large that politicians fear a firestorm of protest and objection. But omitting the numbers will sink the plan just as thoroughly. In Pittsburgh in 1990 when a blue-ribbon group came up with a centennial plan for refurbishing Schenley Plaza in Schenley Park, the $20-million budget so frightened Mayor Sophie Masloff that she forbade anyone in her government from talking about it, put the document in a drawer, and left it for the next mayor to handle. Pittsburgh had financial challenges and she didn't want an outcry from the antispend, antitax crowd. But her action also squelched any possibility of an eruption of excitement from her pro-park constituents. When the next mayor, Tom Murphy, reopened the discussion, a huge swell of public and private activity arose, resulting not only in a beautified Schenley Park but also in the creation of the privately funded Pittsburgh Parks Conservancy, the River Life Task Force, the Three Rivers Trail, the Nine Mile Run Watershed Association, and more.

Let's face it: urban parks are not cheap. It can easily cost three-quarters of a million dollars for a playground. Two million dollars per mile for a rail-trail. Three million for a neighborhood park. Thirty million for a downtown park. But *nothing* urban is cheap. Sports stadiums routinely cost more than $500 million. A highway interchange in Springfield, Virginia, cost more than $1 billion. Fixing the sewer system in Hartford, Connecticut, clocks in at a minimum of $1.6 billion. Burying electrical wiring costs a minimum of $1 million a mile. But costs cannot be hidden. If they are not aired soberly in the master plan, they will be vented drunkenly in later newspaper exposés, talk radio screamfests, and Internet blogging brawls. Worse, if costs are left out of the picture, nothing will happen at all. In modern municipal development, there is no way to get a project started without an appropriation, and there is no appropriation without a budget. What fearful park directors and mayors don't recognize is that the budget—and even the potential opposition aroused by the budget—is what often serves to motivate, unify, and strengthen pro-park activists. The budget elevates the plan from platitude to reality. If the concept is a good one, the stirring up of an opponent should be overmatched by the excitement of two, three, or more supporters. The key to fending off critics, and energizing supporters, is to have a plan so compelling that it's worth the cost. Chicago's Millennium Park, the most expensive U.S. city park ever, did more for the city's image (and probably for its real estate and tourism market) than any other development of the early twenty-first century—not to mention the ripple effect it had in other cities around the country.

It's the same with the timeline. Plans without deadlines do not get implemented. They are continually trumped by other demands that *do* have deadlines. On Earth Day 1994, with great fanfare, the Federal Highway Administration released the National Bicycling and Walking Study. The exhaustive report, three years in the making, set forth the unambiguously numerical goal of doubling the percentage of biking and walking from 7.9 percent to 15.8 percent of all travel trips in the United States. The study caused a sensation in the nonmotorized travel community, and Highway Administrator Rodney E. Slater did more than talk the talk by actually walking the mile from his office to deliver the report to Congress. There was only one fly in the ointment. When a reporter asked Mr. Slater what the deadline was for achieving the goal, he responded, "We actually discussed that issue at great length and ultimately decided that we wouldn't set a deadline. There are just too many variables and unknowns as we move down this road."

A decade later, in a ten-year review of progress and results, the Federal Highway Administration reported that well over $2 billion had been spent on bicycle/pedestrian improvements and that the percentage of journeys by foot and by bike had increased from 7.9 percent to 9.5 percent of all travel trips. Did we do good? *Are* we doing good?

It's impossible to say. At that rate of growth (if it continues), it would take just over forty-nine years to reach the goal. Automobile defenders could express philosophical satisfaction with the measured progress while nonmotorized advocates could scream about the snail's pace, and no one would be right or wrong. Consider the contrast with the electrifying moment on May 25, 1961, when President John F. Kennedy told a joint session of Congress, "I believe that this nation should commit itself to achieving the goal, before this decade is out, of landing a man on the moon and returning him safely to the Earth." (The United States made it with five months to spare.) Or back in 1898 when Theodore Herzl predicted that a Jewish nation would be created within fifty years. (It happened seven months shy of the deadline.) Both of those extremely unlikely events occurred on schedule. In a way, the schedule *made* them happen. Of course, deciding on a timeline requires some underlying reality (we probably couldn't have gotten to the moon in 1962), but soon the timeline itself begins to guide the reality.

A related lesson was learned in Atlanta. In 1993, in preparation for the 1996 Olympics, the city of Atlanta completed a master plan for its park system. The document was as visionary, impressive, and exciting as the city's actual system was lackluster. The only two omissions—purposeful, it turned out—were a timeline and a budget for implementation, and because of them the plan terminally languished. (A plan without a timeline and a budget should more accurately be called a "hope.") The city's single new park during that time, Centennial Olympic Park, was constructed not by the park department but by the Olympics development committee and was later turned over to a state commerce authority.

Eight years later, in 2001, the Center for City Park Excellence released the results of a nationwide study revealing that Atlanta had one of the smallest park systems of any major city, with less land per capita than Tampa, Denver, Houston, Dallas, and many others. As a proportion of city area, Atlanta had less than one-quarter the parkland of Minneapolis or San Diego.

That got attention. There were howls of protest from city boosters, from the business community, even from the mayor's office. Some said that Atlanta, as a "tree city," didn't need as many parks as other places. Or that Atlanta's iconic parks—Piedmont and Grant—are so special that they make up for the shortage. Or that Atlantans can always just hop into their cars and head out to the suburban Chattahoochee River recreation area if they want parks. But through all the twisting, turning, and justifying, the stark statistics rankled. Local park activists used the facts mercilessly and in ways that would have never worked with generalized standards. When Shirley Franklin ran for mayor, she used the data as the basis for campaign pledges. After Franklin was elected she brought in a new park director with a mandate for action and change. Within a few years the Atlanta park system began showing up on "most improved" lists and started being cited for all kinds of innovations—the inauguration of a 22-mile "Beltline" rail-trail loop around downtown; the refurbishment of Piedmont Park by a multimillion-dollar conservancy; the conversion of an old quarry into the largest park in the city; the transformation of a blighted industrial corridor into a mall park between the state capitol and historic Oakland Cemetery park; and more. Simply revealing new facts to a public ready for change played a big role in a paradigm shift in the city's politics.

Last but certainly not least is the evaluation, which closes the circle and leads into the next systemwide master plan five-or-so years later. The evaluation, built into the process in advance, is the ultimate reality check. It's got to be numerical and it has to measure outcomes, not just outputs. Yes, two new recreation centers were constructed on time and on budget, but are they used? How does their use compare with the old recreation centers? Are the users the proper targeted audience? Yes, a park stream corridor was given an ecological upgrade, but did sediment loads in the waterway then actually decline? Was there an increase in the number of fish or fish species? Yes, a ramshackle playground was completely replaced—did that have any effect on home sales, rentals, or property values in the surrounding neighborhood? Did it have any effect on children's obesity rates in the area? Yes, 1,000 new trees were planted. How many survived? Of those that didn't, why not? Yes, a park roadway was closed to auto traffic. Did the amount of weekend recreational cycling increase? How about weekday commuting by bike? Did it have any impact on traffic congestion either inside or outside the park?

The only way to properly answer these and hundreds of other evaluative questions is to determine the baseline in advance. Once the stream is reworked it's too late to find out its old sediment load. Once the road is closed it's too late to measure the old traffic volumes. What is the normal rate of tree mortality? What is the normal use of rec centers? What is the current average body mass index of children? Preplanning the evaluation also helps to ensure that whatever the problem is, the planned project itself is its ideal solution.

In conclusion, master planning, done right, is an enlightening and empowering tool that helps a community identify its needs and desires while also setting a path to achieve results. In contrast, seeking to get there without master planning is much more perilous and often sends communities down one of two dead-end pathways—either seeking blindly to achieve "standards" or relying entirely on a political process that rewards the influential and ignores the powerless.

PART II

Finding Park Space in the City

CHAPTER 11

Buying It

We now move into the reality issue of how to actually find space for parkland in crowded cities.

There is an understandable desire by mayors, city councils, and regular citizens to get parkland for free—by donation, land exchange, no-cost lease, or some other pain-free "silver bullet" solution. And there *are* successful examples of those techniques. But more numerous are cases where a compromise transaction ended up leaving the bullet tarnished—parks ending up in wrong locations or with poor drainage, bad soils, or access problems. The truth is that the most successful way to deal with a shortage of land is to do the obvious: spend some money and buy what is needed. (That's true even if it involves purchasing previously used land that contains dilapidated existing structures or a brownfield that may need cleaning.) Land was purchased for such famous parks as Central Park in New York, Druid Hill Park in Baltimore, Piedmont Park in Atlanta, Post Office Square in Boston, the Burke-Gilman Trail in Seattle, Lykes Gaslight Square Park in Tampa, and Pioneer Courthouse Square in Portland, Oregon. Yes, allocating taxpayer money for parkland can be a political challenge, but it's been done numerous times and is certainly far from impossible. It involves making a convincing case to the public—citing need, showing a vision, explaining benefits, demonstrating payback, and playing to pride. It requires public leadership and also the enthusiastic support of private park advocates. Of course there will always be naysayers and opponents, and at the beginning of any campaign there is always the daunting response by public officials that there is "no money." But in its extensive research on U.S. ballot measures across two decades, The Trust for Public Land has documented that voters overwhelmingly favor spending money on land conservation and parks—whether in fiscally liberal cities like Seattle and San Francisco or tax-averse ones like Colorado Springs and

Dallas (see table 11.1). In 2008 voters said yes to conservation bond measures in Charlotte ($60 million), Tampa ($200 million), San Francisco ($185 million), Seattle ($51 million), Bellevue, Washington ($12 million), Phoenix ($900 million), Santa Fe, New Mexico ($3 million), Arlington, Texas ($2 million), and scores of other smaller places, counties, and states. Interestingly, fluctuations in the economy are not as significant as the popular media make out. In booming times there is more tax revenue available but land costs are high; in recessions, coffers are much barer but land sells for bargain prices. At the depths of the 2009 economic crisis in California, the general manager of the Los Angeles Department of Recreation and Parks was delighted to note that he had millions of unspent dollars in his acquisition account and that prices in the city "haven't been this low in decades."

Chicago is a place where the advantage of buying parkland is understood by the park district and accepted by the citizenry. A classic case occurred in Logan Square, a predominantly Hispanic neighborhood of more than 82,000 on the northwest side. For decades, Logan Square has faced an acute park shortage, needing nearly 100 more acres of parks just to meet Chicago's minimum neighborhood goal of 2 acres for every 1,000 persons. But Logan Square is not the kind of place where a wealthy individual or a well-heeled corporation is likely to donate land. And if the neighborhood has to wait for an inexpensive solution like a land swap or a lucky spinoff from an infrastructure project, it could mean a few more generations of parkless kids. When the political pressure from parents and Friends of the Parks intensified, the Chicago Park District recognized a purchase would be necessary.

The best solution was to expand the existing Haas Park. One of the few unbuilt spaces in Logan Square, 0.86-acre Haas was the only public park available for the 1,300 or so children who lived within a quarter-mile radius. But the district's attempts over the years to expand Haas had all been unsuccessful. Then early in 2004 a warehouse across the street from the park came up for sale. A local community group audaciously suggested purchasing the building, tearing it down, and closing the intervening street. It was not a cheap solution, but it promised to expand the park by 75 percent. The city didn't immediately have funds for the transaction but the superintendent of parks was in favor of the concept. When the seller wouldn't wait a year for an appropriation, The Trust for Public Land stepped in, used its own resources to make

Table 11.1 The Cost of Buying Parkland

Approximate Obligation per Resident per Year from Selected City Referenda on Bond and Tax Measures

City	Year	Mechanism	Parks or Conservation Portion	Population (2006)	Years in Effect	Bond Rating	Imputed Interest Rate	Total for Parks or Conservation, including interest	Approximate Obligation per Resident per Year
San Antonio	2007	Bond	$34,918,450	1,250,996	20	AAA	3%	$46,477,705	$1.86
Los Angeles	2004	Bond	$100,000,000	3,910,145	20	AA	4%	$145,435,279	$1.86
Dallas	2006	Bond	$36,750,000	1,222,260	20	AA+	3.50%	$51,152,447	$2.09
Columbus	2004	Bond	$46,640,000	731,326	20	AAA	3%	$62,079,437	$4.24
Jacksonville	2000	Sales tax	$50,000,000	801,934	10	—	—	$50,000,000	$6.23
San Francisco	2000	Property tax	$150,000,000	750,596	30	—	—	$150,000,000	$6.66
Austin	2006	Bonds (2)	$70,000,000	685,258	20	AAA	3%	$93,172,396	$6.76
Raleigh	2007	Bond	$39,888,721	326,148	20	AAA	3%	$53,093,253	$8.14
Colorado Springs	2003	Sales tax	$60,000,000	370,258	16	—	—	$60,000,000	$10.13
Seattle	2008	Property tax	$50,697,000	573,033	6	—	—	$50,697,000	$14.62
Phoenix	2008	Sales tax	$540,000,000	1,421,284	20	—	—	$540,000,000	$18.94
Charlotte (Mecklenburg County)	2008	Bond	$250,000,000	367,067	20	AAA	3%	$332,758,559	$19.19

Source: Center for Conservation Finance, The Trust for Public Land

the purchase, and held the land (and paid the taxes) for two years. When the park district got its appropriation, it bought the land from TPL, removed the structure, had the street closed, and built the park addition. Haas Park, now 1.54 acres, is still small but it was large enough in versatile Chicago to host a flag football program, a 200-youth soccer league, a movie festival, a health fair, picnics, and a karate demonstration in its first year of operation.

A much larger land purchase occurred in 1995 when a 50-acre railyard came up for sale in downtown Santa Fe, New Mexico. Santa Fe, although the state capital, is a small, low-rise city that prides itself on its arts, architecture, multicultural history, and walkable scale and pace. It is also fast-growing, and the potential misappropriation of the railyard had many residents concerned. Everyone recognized the importance of the central location, and there was also strong agitation for a focal park, but the property was appraised at a daunting $26 million. Ultimately, after months of complex dealing, the Trust for Public Land negotiated the price down to $21 million, bought it, and resold it to the city. Santa Fe covered part of the cost with available capital funds and the other part by issuing new revenue bonds backed by tax receipts. The city then reserved 13 acres for a major park and leased the remaining land to commercial tenants to cover the costs of the entire property. (Following that, TPL separately embarked on an arduous $13-million fundraising effort to pay for the construction of the park, which did not finally open until 2008.) In the final analysis the Railyard Park was a $34-million creation for which, at the outset, there was "no money" available.

Even Dallas, which for years did not regularly invest in parks, found that it can suddenly shift gears. In the mid-1990s, for internal business reasons, the Boeing Corporation decided to move its headquarters and 500 of its top staff from Washington State to a more geographically central location. After exhaustive analysis and negotiations, the choice was narrowed to the cities of Denver, Chicago, and Dallas. In 2001 Boeing chose Chicago. Among other reasons, the company believed that Chicago offered its executives a higher quality of life. Besides world-class music, art, theater, and food, of course, Chicago had been greening its lakefront for well over a century and had been building neighborhood parks and field houses throughout the city for decades.

The bad news hit Dallas like a bombshell. Park advocates, who had been complaining unsuccessfully about the quantity and quality of the city's downtown parks and about the lack of park spending, spun into action. They pressed the city's corporate and political leadership about the economic necessity of a serious investment in parks. The park department, which for years had been squeezed, was suddenly given a generous budget for an ambitious "Renaissance Plan." Four years later, in 2006, a referendum on a huge park bond was held, and it overwhelmingly passed. The result was an infusion of nearly $45 million for land acquisition (along with more than $55 million for a multitude of improvements to existing parks). Land that had formerly been turned down as unaffordable and a waste of money was suddenly in play as an investment in a greater city—three acres to create Pacific Plaza from former parking lots and rundown buildings ($9 million); a deck park on top of the Woodall Rodgers Freeway ($20 million, to be matched by twice as much from other sources); 100 acres of new parks and trails in residential neighborhoods; not to mention replacing 245 outdated playgrounds ($36 million) and restoring Fair Park to its former splendor ($100 million).

Dallas Parks and Recreation Director Paul Dyer analyzed the turnaround. "Back in what I call the 'bad old days,'" he said, "we had so little support we were terrified to even ask for the one-and-a-half million it would take to do a master plan. But we had to do it—we had to figure out how to even start the process. So we did an inventory of our system—every barbeque pit, every jogging trail, everything. Then we held community meetings to ask people what they wanted. We found that, essentially, the emperor had no clothes—the Dallas park system was way behind where people claimed it was. It was scary to stand up and say it, but we had no place to go but up. Then when the Boeing situation hit, everything changed. There was suddenly money and we were ready to implement the Renaissance Plan."

In fact, despite the claims of "no money," cities of all fiscal stripes—from booming to reeling—have dug down and purchased parkland. St. Louis used some revenue it had from a land lease to buy two vacant parcels for neighborhood parks in 2008. Los Angeles, frequently criticized for being park-poor in its more crowded neighborhoods, acquired 408 acres between 2005 and 2009 for eighteen new parks and the expansion of eight existing ones. Supercrowded Miami spent $6.6 million of its Florida Communities Trust funds on a 6-acre addition to

Table 11.2   Developer Exactions
Land or Financial Payment Required of Developers for Parks, Selected Cities

City	Approximate Amount of Land Required from Developers (acres per 1,000 new residents)	Approximate Payment Rate in Lieu of Land (Dollars per 1,000 new residents)
Austin	5	n.a.
Chicago	1.7	$313,000
Columbus, Ohio	5.5	varies
Fort Worth	6.25*	$200,000**
Long Beach, Calif.	1.35	$1,000,000
Portland, Ore.	4.56	$500,000
San Antonio	4	n.a.
San Jose, Calif.	3	n.a.

* plus $30,000 per acre
** in center city
n.a.—not available
Source: Center for City Park Excellence, The Trust for Public Land

Fern Isle Park in 2008. Columbus, Ohio, spent about $3 million on 98 acres of neighborhood parks in 2007 and then turned around and spent another $2.1 million the following year on a major park and a greenway. Las Vegas between 2006 and 2008 spent $8 million on four properties for Douglas Selby Park and to expand the existing Las Vegas Wash Trail and Park.

Some cities have another option for park dollars. Atlanta; Chicago; Portland, Oregon; Columbus, Ohio; and many cities in Texas and California require developers to provide parkland in conjunction with the housing they are constructing (see table 11.2). The theory is twofold. First, since many new developments remove private green open space from the region's inventory, providing parks is partial compensation. Second, since new houses mean more people, these new residents need facilities so that they don't overburden existing parks. The land (or in-lieu cash payment, which most developers prefer) is on a per-housing-unit basis and can quickly become significant in fast-growing areas. Between 1986 and 2000, Austin used its developer fees to buy 867 acres for parks. Fort Worth, which grew by about 11,000 residents per year in the 1990s and 2000s, added 712 acres through developer exactions. Portland, Oregon, where the fee is called a "system development charge," cleverly used anticipated development revenue as a guaranteed source of income, allowing the city to sell bonds; by using bond revenue upfront (and repaying it later using the developers' fees), Portland was able to quickly purchase 91 acres in places of expected population growth before property values had risen.

There are many imperfections in the developer exaction process, the worst being that the fees are rarely high enough to fully cover the cost of land. Also, courts have been very strict about guaranteeing "nexus"— reasonable distance between houses and purchased parkland, again reducing the chance of finding affordable land. But it is one more tool in the funding toolbox. And, regardless of fluctuations in the housing market, developer exactions are growing in importance because of the depth and breadth of the antitax movement in many communities. Even Houston finally stood up to its powerful and recalcitrant developer community and, in 2008, passed its first exaction law. Other cities with weak regulations already on the books, including Atlanta and Miami, are seeking to strengthen them.

CHAPTER 12

Utilizing Urban Redevelopment

On a grander scale than buying an individual parcel of land is the redevelopment of a large former institutional site. Opportunities for urban parks keep opening up in old downtowns because of what Toronto architect and urban designer Ken Greenberg evocatively calls "the retreat of the industrial glacier." In the rare case, an entire property might become a park; more commonly, parks can be interspersed with new housing, offices, shops, and public buildings (see table 12.1). Redevelopment is the fact of life that disproves the common, thoughtless remark, "Our city is all built out, so there is no room for more parks." Cities change all the time and every change holds opportunity. If there is room for a single new building, or even a new parking lot, there is room for a new park, as has been seen recently in Kansas City (Ilus Davis Park), Cleveland (Whiskey Island), San Francisco (Visitacion Valley), Washington, D.C. (Canal Park), and Newark, New Jersey (Nat Turner Park).

As seeds for the regrowth, parks are key. But they must be reserved, designed, and placed in advance of the built environment that will surround them. Unfortunately, putting parks first doesn't come naturally in the United States—too often they consist of the occasional misshapen parcels of leftover space with steep slopes, poor drainage, or other problems. Making a park the centerpiece of a project requires a city with sophisticated planning capabilities, strong regulations, and an engaged citizenry with the willpower to demand excellence.

Redevelopment can take several forms. Sometimes a large industrial owner goes bankrupt or otherwise vacates a site, which is then acquired by a public agency for either total or partial park use. This is what happened with two rail yards in downtown Los Angeles, a steel mill in Chicago, an oil storage depot in Seattle, a ferry terminal in New York, a quarry in Atlanta, a railroad track in Washington, D.C., and hundreds

Table 12.1 Second Time Around
Selected Parks Created by Urban Redevelopment Agencies

City	Park	Agency/Authority	Acres	Cost	Year Completed
Los Angeles	Grand Hope Park	Los Angeles Community Redevelopment Agency	2.5	n.a.	1994
Portland	South Waterfront Park	Portland Development Commission	4.31	$7,000,000	1999
San Francisco	Rincon Park	San Francisco Redevelopment Agency	2	$4,000,000	2003
San Francisco	Mission Bay Parks (first 3)	San Francisco Redevelopment Agency	6.2	$12,300,000	2004
Las Vegas	Centennial Plaza	Las Vegas Redevelopment Agency	0.75	$350,000	2005
San Jose	Bellevue Park	Redevelopment Agency of City of San Jose	1.75	$6,500,000	2006
San Diego	City Heights Square	Mission Valley Flood Channel	1.14	n.a.	2007
Albuquerque	Sawmill Park and Trail	Metropolitan Redevelopment Agency	1.2	n.a.	2008
Seattle	High Point Parks (several)	Seattle Housing Authority	21	n.a.	2008

n.a. not available
Source: Center for City Park Excellence, The Trust for Public Land

of other facilities elsewhere. A variant on this is the decommissioning of a large governmental holding and its conversion to park use, as was done with military bases in San Francisco (the Presidio) and Seattle (Fort Lawton, now Discovery Park), airports in Denver (Stapleton Airport, now the Stapleton neighborhood with numerous parks) and Chicago (Meigs Field, now Northerly Island Park), a highway in Portland, Oregon (Harbor Drive, now Tom McCall Waterfront Park), and a prison farm in Memphis (Shelby Farms, now Shelby Farms Park).

Atlanta is the site of one of the greatest repurposing of industrial lands into a multipurpose greenway/transitway. Conceived in 1988 and begun in 2002, the Atlanta Beltline will, when completed, consist of a 22-mile trail-and-transit facility completely encircling downtown with badly needed green space. Projected for completion by 2030, the Beltline will cost about $2.5 billion and is expected to create as much as $20 billion in new value from the dwellings, office parks, and commercial establishments that are springing up because of it.

A less grandiose but more immediately successful development already operates in the Pearl District in Portland, Oregon, where the city's redevelopment agency set aside 7 acres for three different parks among a raft of new lofts and apartments on an old rail yard. Unlike most new in-town infill developments, the Pearl District is bouncing with children and young families, most of whom can be seen in the new park's fountain on nice days.

A city may identify a blighted neighborhood, delineate it a redevelopment area, and attempt to remake it with new zoning and incentives, mixing a public park and private housing projects. That's what St. Paul, Minnesota, did with its downtown Wacouta Commons project, two acres of parkland among new mixed-style and mixed-price housing in a neighborhood previously consisting mostly of parking lots. As obvious and "normal" as Wacouta Commons might sound, that combination—downtown mixed-price housing combined with a full-fledged park—is remarkably rare in twenty-first-century urban America; it's a combination known as "Smart Collaboration," and much more of it is desperately needed.

The holy grail of renewal is along a shoreline, whether stream, river, lake, or sea. There is simply nothing like water to add interest, romance, and value. But it's a contentious zone because of the competition between public and private access. Apartment owners, of course, love having undistracted views of a stream, pond, or harbor; but the city's other residents also want that view, that breeze, that opportunity. At the very least they want to walk and bike along the edge—if not also to have space to fish, boat, picnic, sunbathe, play sports, attend concerts, and otherwise enjoy the ambience. The tug-of-war comes down literally to feet and inches. Does the public get merely a sterile, 10-foot paved walkway, or 20 feet with a grassy margin, or 40 feet with separate trails for walking and bikes, or 100 feet with real space for decent trees and attractive landscaping, or 200 feet to include a lawn area for throwing a Frisbee or putting down a blanket and a picnic basket? The more vigorous the debate, the healthier.

Once a wall of office or apartment buildings rises up to separate citizens from a river—as occurred years ago on parts of the Chicago River in Chicago—it is almost impossible to recoup the public's loss. (Fortunately, Chicago has been working to atone for its past errors. In the 1980s it began negotiating voluntary setbacks along all inland waterways, and in 1998 it adopted a requirement that any new construction on the Chicago River have a minimum 30-foot setback.)

In 2008 Mayor Richard M. Daley undertook a major urban redevelopment project on his *other* waterfront, Lake Michigan, when Meigs Field, a noncommercial airport on an artificial island, was acquired. The city tore out the runways and converted it into Northerly Island Park. The new 90-acre park, designed with plenty of community input, has hiking and bicycling trails, a concert venue, a nature center in the old terminal building, and a wintertime exhibit area about sled dogs and wolves. The peninsula is dedicated in particular to birders and birds—the Chicago Park District offers visitors birdwatching packets (complete with loaner binoculars for children and others), and there is also a satellite hospital of the Flint Creek Wildlife Center for any feathered creature injured crashing into the glass skyscrapers of the nearby downtown. But most alluring is the silence so close to the city. "If you face west, you have a spectacular view of the skyline. If you face east, the expanse of water goes on forever," says Gia Biagi, director of planning and development for the Chicago Park District. "And either way you are struck by the quiet."

Denver has become a leader of the parks-as-seeds-of-redevelopment movement. When the city built a new airport and slated the old one for conversion into the new neighborhood of Stapleton, it crafted a comprehensive requirement for all kinds of parks—wildlands, playgrounds, ornamental boulevards, greenways, and playing fields—1,100 acres of them, almost one-quarter of the entire property. Denver allocated $46 million to get the ball rolling, including 80-acre Central Park at Stapleton, and developers were required to provide the rest. Stapleton is today considered one of the most successful (and profitable) infill "new urbanist" developments, and it is the most park-rich. (New Urbanism, the movement to recapture the denser, rectilinear, walkable, front-porch-oriented development style of nineteenth-century urban America, is unfortunately not often known for its great parks.) A couple of miles west is another Denver redevelopment success, Commons Park, which is part of the total renewal of the Central Platte River Valley. The 22-

acre park, built on an old rail yard, has helped entice the development of more than 2,000 units of housing in a part of town that just a few years earlier was feared and shunned.

But if redevelopment parks are only included as an afterthought in a project, their roles and profile within the community can be substantially diminished. Atlantic Station, a muscular and ambitious redevelopment in Midtown Atlanta, is a case in point. Atlantic Station was a groundbreaking concept for reclaiming the contaminated remains of a former steel mill—this in a metropolitan area where development normally leapfrogs over problem properties to sprawl ever deeper into the exurbs. The effort was given strong backing by Governor Roy Barnes and has earned awards from both the Environmental Protection Agency and the Sierra Club. The developers capped the entire 138-acre property to seal in any contamination, followed some of the new urbanist design principles, linked the community to existing transit, and used both energy-efficient building technology and water-saving stormwater control technology. There are even three parks totalling 11 acres, about 8 percent of the land area. But it is obvious that planning for the parks came last. The largest one consists of a narrow ring of steeply sloping land surrounding a stormwater detention pond and encircled by a fence. It's got a pretty pedestrian bridge but it is not usable for anything other than gazing at the water. Next is a small linear park with an allée of trees that doesn't connect anything and is being held for possible conversion to a trolley corridor if and when ridership projections work out. The smallest, named Central Park, consists of two tiny squares of grass, readily programmable for event use but uninspiring—almost unnoticeable—on their own. Much of Atlantic Station has the look and feel of a large, outdoor shopping mall surrounded by tall steel-and-glass office and apartment buildings, and its Central Park feels like the mall's center plaza where a balloon-folding man and a character from Sesame Street might show up on schedule every hour. It is obvious that at full build-out, Atlantic Station's 10,000 or so residents will need to use other offsite parkland elsewhere in the city.

Photo A. The Capital Crescent Trail as it enters Bethesda, Maryland, 7 miles from its starting point in Washington, D.C. A converted railroad track, the Capital Crescent serves more than 1 million recreational and purposeful cyclists, skaters, runners, and walkers every year. Already, 15,000 miles of abandoned rail corridors have been converted to linear parks. For more on rail trails, see chapter 16. (Photo by Barbara Richey, courtesy Rails-to-Trails Conservancy.)

Photo B. Not all cemeteries are parks, but Oakland Cemetery in downtown Atlanta certainly is—it's owned and operated by the Atlanta Department of Parks and Recreation. Thousands of acres of urban cemetery lands could potentially be put to more park-like uses. For more on cemeteries as parks, see chapter 21. (Photo by Joey Ivansco.)

Photo C. Community gardens aren't full-fledged parks, but in crowded neighborhoods they exhibit a lot of park attributes. Not only does the Central Bainbridge St. Community Garden produce thousands of pounds of vegetables, it also serves as a hub of activity in Brooklyn's Bedford-Stuyvesant community. For more on community gardens, see chapter 13. (Photo by Avery Wham.)

Photos D & E. For more than a century Cool Spring Reservoir in Wilmington, Delaware, was open to the air but surrounded by a fence (right). In 2009, responding to a new pure-water law, the city buried the reservoir in a concrete tank, covered it with a grassy field, added an ornamental pond (of nondrinking water), and—voila!—found itself with new parkland. The photo (bottom) was taken a month before opening day. For more on covering reservoirs with parks, see chapter 19. (Photos by Philip Franks, Hurley-Franks and Assocs., top; and Rory MacRory, AECOM, bottom.)

Photos F & G. The schoolyard of P.S. 221 in Crown Heights, Brooklyn, prior to renovation (above) and after on a summer day in August 2009 (below), thanks to a partnership among the New York City Department of Education, the New York City Department of Parks and Recreation, and the Trust for Public Land. For more on schoolyard parks, see chapter 18. (Photos by Julieth Rivera, above; and Joan Keener, below.)

Photo H. Not your usual city street, Boston's Commonwealth Avenue is in the finest tradition of urban boulevards, providing art, horticulture, recreation, and significant added value to the homes on either side. For more on boulevards and parkways, see chapter 22. (Photo by Swampyank via Wikipedia Creative Commons.)

Photo I. By decking over a portion of Interstate 35, Duluth, Minnesota, was able to save its Rose Garden and provide a park connection directly to its Lake Superior waterfront. Outdoor-oriented Duluth has more highway deck parks than any other city of its size. For more on decking highways, see chapter 23. (Photo courtesy Minnesota Department of Transportation.)

Photo J. NCNB Plaza in Tampa, the nation's first "rooftop park" when it opened in 1988. Other parks had been built over buried parking lots, but this one—designed by Landscape Architect Dan Kiley and sometimes called Kiley Garden—was the first elevated off the ground. Because of water drainage and other issues, the park has since been completely rebuilt. For more on rooftop parks, see chapter 17. (Photo by Aaron Kiley.)

Photo K. The aptly named Mt. Trashmore in Virginia Beach, Virginia. The city's highest point and its largest non-wetland park, Mt. Trashmore was constructed in 1974 over an 800-foot-high mound of municipal refuse and became the best known of the nation's early landfill parks. For more on landfill parks, see chapter 14. (Photo by Backus Aerial.)

Photos L & M. Originally the grand entranceway to Pittsburgh's Schenley Park, Schenley Plaza was lost to automobile storage (above) for sixty years beginning in 1948. Under pressure from the Pittsburgh Parks Conservancy, it was completely rebuilt and returned to the people in 2008 (below). For more on reducing parking in parks, see chapter 25. (Photos by LaQuatra Bonci Associates, above; and Melissa McMasters, below.)

Photo N. Training wheels, scooters, and a first-time two-wheel pedaler in Atlanta's Piedmont Park—with nary an automobile to worry about. For more on closing roads and streets to cars, see chapter 24. (Photo courtesy Piedmont Park Conservancy.)

Photo O. Many developments have functional water detention basins, but few have gone as far as Seattle's new High Point housing development in turning them into attractive, people-oriented spaces. The development's Viewpoint Park has an overlook, trails, benches, a playground, and an artificial boulder-strewn stream. For more on stormwater parks, see chapter 15. (Photo courtesy Seattle Housing Authority.)

Photo P. The Railyard Park in Santa Fe, New Mexico, features a farmers' market, playground, sprayground, trail, labyrinth, and many other amenities. Most visitors don't realize that it was constructed on a cleaned-up former industrial property. For more on utilizing urban redevelopment for parks, see chapter 12. (Photo by Don J. Usner.)

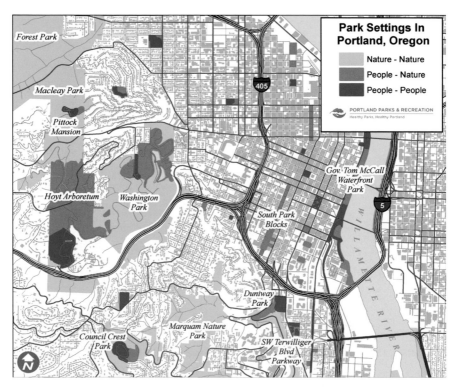

Photo Q. The city of Portland, Oregon, is pioneering a new way of classifying parkland, dropping the concept of "active" and "passive" in favor of settings and uses. Even in the near-downtown area there are parks that range from intense people-to-people spaces through people-in-nature places to almost wilderness nature-to-nature tracts. And some parks have more than one classification. For more on classifying parkland, see chapter 2. (Map courtesy Bureau of Parks and Recreation, City of Portland, Oregon.)

CHAPTER 13

Community Gardens

Community gardens are a vastly underappreciated and underprovided resource for cities, both at ground level and on rooftops. As reported by University of Illinois Landscape Architecture Professor Laura Lawson in her excellent book *City Bountiful*, surveys from the 1970s and 1980s revealed that while gardening was Americans' favorite outdoor leisure activity, somewhere between 7 million and 18 million people wanted to garden but weren't able to because they did not have the space. With today's higher population, including millions of immigrants who live in cities but still have deep cultural attachments to agriculture, the situation is now unquestionably more severe. In a nation engulfed by profligate use of land, the irony is hard to miss. Americans traveling in urban areas overseas are often struck by the fact that even small patches alongside railroad tracks and roads, and odd plots between buildings—spaces that are almost invariably wasted in the United States—are intensively cultivated for flowers, vegetables, and spices. In most European countries trains routinely pass hundreds of garden plots in the several miles between city centers and true farm fields on the outskirts.

Community gardens do not have full-fledged pedigrees as parks, but they are certainly members of the extended family, and they are overwhelmingly urban. Coming in a diversity of forms, they can provide beauty, supply food, educate youth, build confidence, reduce pesticide exposure, grow social capital, preserve mental health, instill pride, and raise property values. Although the number of community gardens in the United States is not known, a 1996 survey of thirty-eight major cities by the American Community Gardening Association revealed 6,020 gardens, and the national total may be three times that. In 2008, The Trust for Public Land's survey of the park systems of the seventy-seven largest cities revealed 682 gardens (and 12,988 individual garden plots) specifically owned by park departments and located on urban parkland.

The national movement has a great deal of exuberant vitality, demonstrated even by place names and their fostering organizations: the Garden of Eatin', Queen Pea Garden, Harlem Rose Garden, Jes' Good Rewards Children's Garden, Paradise on Earth, Garden Resources of Washington (GROW), Denver Urban Gardens (DUG), Boston Urban Gardeners (BUG), San Francisco League of Urban Gardeners (SLUG), and Los Angeles' Gardening Angels. But the movement is also severely underfunded, poorly organized, and subject to a bruisingly high level of burnout and turnover. (GROW, SLUG, and BUG have all gone out of business.) Put simply, between the legalities, the neighbors, and the typical challenges of soil and weather, urban agriculture is extraordinarily difficult, even more difficult than running normal public parks.

Vegetables, fruits, and flowers require protection from theft or inadvertent damage, and this entails unsightly fences and unneighborly locks. Because of this, gardens require close control and, in some cities, end up being rationed by way of waiting lists and small fees. Finally, community gardens have a particular look that is very much in the eye of the beholder. For every wannabe farmer who delights in seeing rows of seedlings, pyramids of compost, a shock of vegetable stakes, and dripping irrigation hoses, there is a City Beautiful purist who laments the unkempt prospect and the loss of a potential manicured lawn. On the other hand, the gardeners with their planting, watering, weed-pulling, and harvesting are the everyday users who can help make a park more inviting, busier, and safer. Plus, community gardens make extremely efficient use of space. An area that could barely fit a single tennis court might hold 75 garden plots; a soccer field might be replaced with 300 or more. Moreover, gardens can be placed close to streets and railroads because they have no errant balls bouncing into traffic.

Depending on a host of external factors, the demand for community gardens fluctuates like a pendulum. Every economic downturn sees people trying to save money by growing their own (and then often reverting to supermarket simplicity when good times return). Same with pesticide scares—each frightening headline drives a few more people off "the agro-chemical grid," though it doesn't always last. Most recently, the new interest in saving energy by eating locally has made some easterners and northerners swear off produce from places like California,

Arizona, and Florida. All these factors could spur a renaissance in park gardens, particularly if troublesome ownership and management issues can be solved.

For the purposes of this book, there are two major classes of community gardens: those within existing parks and stand-alone gardens that have sprung up in vacant spaces. The former group does not, of course, represent an increase in the overall park acreage in a city, but it sometimes puts existing parkland to a higher-intensity use or otherwise improves it. The latter effectively increases the size of a city's system of parks and park-like spaces. There are numerous opportunities for an enormous expansion of both kinds of garden lands.

Most cities have plenty of underused or even unused chunks of parks that could be developed into community gardens. Even super crowded places like Jersey City and San Francisco have parkland that is essentially unvisited. That doesn't automatically mean it's perfect for gardening—it may be too shady or too deep within a big park to be reachable by potential gardeners—but those drawbacks might be fixable through tree trimming or park redesign. Chances are that underused "backwater" park areas became that way because they are frightening or have safety issues that need to be dealt with comprehensively, and a garden might be one piece of the larger revival puzzle. Gardens need to be near edges where they can be seen and where people, vehicles, and irrigation water can easily reach them. But putting a garden near an edge helps open up the next internal ring of the park to greater use, thus gradually reclaiming what might be a no-man's land in the interior. There is no guarantee that the dozens of challenging factors that make for a successful community garden—leadership, community involvement, well-enforced rules, adequate funding, stable management, good soil, sufficient sun and water, and much more—can all be provided within a city park by a city park department. But overall, official park department gardens are more stable (if perhaps also a bit more staid) than stand-alone gardens operated on vacant lots by community groups and land trusts.

On the other hand, putting a community garden into an existing park could well mean not putting in a soccer field, dog park, or memorial grove that some other constituency wants. Thus, developing a new, stand-alone community garden leaves existing parkland unmolested and raises the tide for everyone. (It also provides a boost to home values in the surrounding community; a 2007 study by the New York University Furman Center for Real Estate and Urban Policy found that gardens in New York's poorest neighborhoods lifted property values by up to 9.4 percent after five years.) Opportunities abound. Buffalo, St. Louis, Detroit, Cleveland, and Pittsburgh—all of them less than half as populated as they were in 1950—contain thousands of vacant lots, many municipally owned because of nonpayment of taxes. Even in less hard-hit places like Chicago and Kansas City, or resurgent places like Atlanta, New York, Denver, and Seattle, there are still numerous gaps in the urban fabric that are doing little more than collecting cars, weeds, and garbage.

Of the 18,000 or however many community gardens, most of them stand-alone gardens, the great majority operate in humble, contented obscurity, providing their microfarmers with fruits for the eye or the stomach, sociality for the heart, and pleasant breathing spaces for the neighborhood. But every now and then, an issue flares. In both New York in the late 1990s and Los Angeles in the early 2000s community garden battles became front-page showdowns, complete with rallies, arrests, Hollywood celebrities, and multimillion-dollar fundraising campaigns. In Seattle, thanks in part to the P-Patch Trust, a formal land trust that owns land and does organizing, gardeners defeated an effort to convert a longstanding garden into a golf course driving range. But the average urban gardener is a libertarian communalist, happy to share her tiny piece of green earth with compatriots but also happy to not be bothered.

This is actually a problem. Without robust engagement in politics and the public process, gardeners do not bring themselves into the park's mainstream. They regularly become trapped in the romantic but vicious cycle now found in many ramshackle neighborhoods with numerous abandoned properties in legal limbo: stand-alone gardens are created entrepreneurially and extralegally; the gardens receive support from civic-minded nonprofits and begin to generate buzz; artists, gay people, and other urban pioneers discover the area; developers promote the trend; middle-class professionals move in; demand expands; construction swells; gardens are bulldozed.

A community garden program cannot be left to operate reactively. It must be designed to protect gardens at the beginning of the process, not at the end. Gardens must be clearly recognized as an integral part of a city's park system, and they should be included in all redevelopment projects—particularly those that are high-density and that are marketed to former suburbanites who may love all aspects of the city except its lack of gardening space. This is surprisingly rare. Even Arlington, Virginia, poster community of the smart growth movement with scores of new high-rises along its Rosslyn-Ballston subway line, has not created a single new community garden for the 20,000 or so residents who have flocked there in the past thirty years. (The county has responded by dividing many garden plots in half, but the waiting time to get a garden in Arlington is still three to four years.)

As of 2009, the only city that has a truly sophisticated garden structure is Seattle. Chicago, New York, Philadelphia, and several other places have relatively strong private-sector agencies or public-private partnerships that own, hold, and support significant numbers of community gardens, but only Seattle's P-Patch program proactively plans, sites, negotiates, sets rules, and protects gardens throughout the city. P-Patch, which began in 1973 and was named after Rainie Picardo, the farmer who first allowed residents to begin gardening on his land, once even counted as a gardening member Mayor Wes Uhlman. Today P-Patch has sixty-eight gardens, an annual budget of $650,000, and a staff of six, and Seattle has more garden plots per capita than any other major city. Even more impressive, Seattle's City Council passed a formal resolution supporting community gardens and recommending their colocation on other city-owned property. The city's comprehensive plan calls for a standard of one garden for every 2,000 households in high-density neighborhoods (known in Seattle as "urban villages"). Nevertheless, despite this abundance, P-Patch still has a waiting list of 1,900 persons; in crowded neighborhoods that translates to three to four years.

Finding a numerical balance between houses and gardens is tricky. Moribund neighborhoods drowning in vacant lots certainly benefit from greening programs, but it would be shortsighted to lock in every temporary garden in perpetuity. These neighborhoods frankly need economic vitality and the increase in population and buildings that accompanies it. Conversely, economically overheated neighborhoods are tremendous revenue and tax drivers for the city, but politicians need to make sure that these "golden goose" places aren't overbuilt and eventually suffocated by their growth.

Stand-alone gardens need not be slotted only to old home sites. One particularly promising locale is along rail lines, both abandoned and active. Community gardens have already been created alongside the Washington and Old Dominion Railroad Trail in Arlington, Virginia; the Ohlone Trail in Berkeley, California; and the Capital City Trail in Madison, Wisconsin. In Queens, New York, the Long Island City Roots Garden was created directly over the tracks of the unused-but-not-abandoned Degnon Terminal Railroad. (To prevent official abandonment the railroad required that the tracks be retained, so the gardeners bulldozed out 140 cubic yards of garbage and covered the rails with 160 cubic yards of clean dirt; the garden is a train-shaped 26 feet wide and 145 feet long.)

While gardens alongside rail trails are fine, they don't actually increase the amount of parkland in a city. To do that requires moving up to the next level: creating community gardens alongside *nonabandoned* rail lines. This is a tougher challenge but has an added benefit since there are few parts of a city less attractive than the edges of a railroad. From Philadelphia to Los Angeles, as dumping grounds for all manner of modern detritus, the edges of urban rail corridors provide depressing vistas for train riders and local residents alike. Some analysts are convinced that rail ridership would jump up a few notches solely if the view was pleasanter. Back in the 1960s, Lady Bird Johnson spearheaded the remarkably successful highway beautification program, but no subsequent first lady (or anyone else) has taken on what might today be called an extreme track makeover program. Could gardens lead the way?

Because of railroad industry reluctance and disinterest, bolstered by issues of liability and a generally impenetrable bureaucracy, the number of agreements between railroads and gardeners in the United States is very small. For a time there was a market garden alongside tracks in Baltimore, but when the B&O Railroad Museum decided to expand, the garden was removed. For several years in the late 1980s the Pennsylvania Horticultural Society had a "Ribbon of Gold" competition whereby railroads would get a prize for planting fields of yellow flowers alongside active lines, but that ultimately evolved into other programs, and Philadelphia's many tracks reverted to eyesore status.

One notable success is in Madison, Wisconsin, where the St. Paul Avenue Garden operates under a license with the Wisconsin Central

Railroad, a subsidiary of Canadian National Railways. The line is lightly used by low-speed freight traffic, so there is not even a fence alongside the tracks. The 72-plot, 25-foot-wide garden runs for about two blocks in an intense utility corridor that includes a buried fiber-optic cable and an overhead high-tension line. "It used to be a dumping ground sort of place," explained Joe Mathers, garden specialist with the Community Action Coalition for South Central Wisconsin. "Then, in the early 1980s Madison got a lot of Hmong refugees from Southeast Asia so we started looking for land for them to farm. We were in a recession so there was land available. When the economy improved development resumed and we lost some spaces. But we should always be able to hang on to this garden—nothing is permitted to be built here."

There are a scattering of community gardens alongside rail lines in Chicago, some consisting of flower gardens to beautify station areas, and there is a garden in the Bronx, New York, alongside a large railroad storage yard. In both those cities, the rail owners are public agencies—Metra and the MTA, respectively. Public rail agencies may be more amenable to leasing or licensing trackside space than private train operators, although no detailed study of opportunities has yet been carried out.

CHAPTER 14

Old Landfills

New parks can be fashioned out of old garbage dumps. It's not as bad as it sounds.

International Balloon Park in Albuquerque, Cesar Chavez Park in Berkeley, McAlpine Creek Soccer Complex in Charlotte, Red Rock Canyon Open Space in Colorado Springs, Rogers Park Golf Course in Tampa, and hundreds of others, both famous and obscure, have been created from landfills (see table 14.1). And in a few more years New York City's 2,200-acre Fresh Kills Landfill will have settled in to become that city's largest park.

Landfill parks go back to at least 1916 (many years before the word "landfill" was coined) when the old Rainier Dump in Seattle was turned into the Rainier Playfield. In 1935 in that same city a more momentous conversion transformed the 62-acre Miller Street Dump into a portion of the now-famous Washington Park Arboretum. The following year, New York City closed the putrid Corona Dumps—famously called the "Valley of Ashes" by F. Scott Fitzgerald in *The Great Gatsby*—and began preparing the land for construction of the 1939 World's Fair. Following World War II, as the volume of trash in America mushroomed, so did the number of landfills. The U.S. Environmental Protection Agency (EPA) estimates that as many as 3,500 landfills have closed since 1991; the number from earlier years is anyone's guess.

In an ideal world all trash would be recycled and there would be no landfills. But in a time of severe urban space and resource constraints, closed landfills represent excellent locales for three big reasons: size, location, and cost. A former dump is usually one of the few large, open locations within a dense metro area. There is also the opportunity to correct what may have been a longstanding environmental injustice to the surrounding residents. Finally, there's a good chance that the

Table 14.1 Garbage In, Park Out

Selected Parks Constructed on Former Landfills

City	Name	Year Completed	Acres	Cost	Amenities
Albuquerque	Kodak Albuquerque Int'l. Balloon Fiesta	n.a.	78	n.a.	Hot Air Balloon Fiesta
Austin	Mabel Davis Park	2004	50	n.a.	Skate park, pool, ball fields, fishing
Boston	Millennium Park	2000	100	$30,000,000	Sports fields, boat ramp, trails
Boston	Spectacle Island	n.a.	121	n.a.	Marina
Charlotte	Southside Park	1998	11	n.a.	Basketball, playing fields, playground
Chicago	Harborside Golf Center	1996	450	$30,000,000	Golf courses
Colorado Springs	Red Rock Canyon Open Space	2004	789	$12,500,000	Trails
Columbus	Phoenix Golf Links	2000	185	n.a.	Golf course
Fresno	Regional Sports Park	2003	350	$8,000,000	Sports fields, lake
Jacksonville	Earl M. Johnson Memorial Park	1990	56	n.a.	Fishing lakes, soccer fields
New York	Gateway National Park	n.a.	400	$200,000,000	Trails, bay observation
Oakland	Metropolitan Golf Links	2003	125	n.a.	Golf course
Sacramento	Sutter's Landing Regional Park	n.a.	172	n.a.	Skate park, trails, waterfront
San Antonio	Pearsall Park	n.a.	232	n.a.	Dog park, skate park, trails
San Jose	Martin Park	2007	6	$1,100,000	Sports fields, jogging, picnic area
Seattle	Rainier Playfield	1910	10	n.a.	Play area, tennis, picnic area
St. Louis	W.C. Handy Park	1941	12	n.a.	Softball, football, basketball, playground
Tampa	Ace Golf Driving Range	1999	15	n.a.	Driving range
Virginia Beach	Mount Trashmore	1974	50	n.a.	Lake, playground, skate park, trails

n.a.—not available

Source: Center for City Park Excellence, The Trust for Public Land

landfill—which may be as small as dozens of acres or as large as 1,000 or more—is free or inexpensive to buy or possibly that it even comes with its own supporting funds.

While a capped landfill is not necessarily a park director's first choice for a parcel of land, it's impressive and instructive that so many perfectly adequate—or even better than adequate—city parks started out as dumps. Communities from coast to coast have been jumping at the chance to use them. Based on a survey, the Center for City Park Excellence estimates that there may already be as many as 4,500 acres of landfill parks in major U.S. cities.

In Portland, Oregon, the park department is getting a free 25-acre park. All closure and conversion costs for Cully Park were paid by the solid waste department, which built up a reserve for exactly that purpose by charging a per-ton fee on garbage disposed there. (The park department coordinates closely in habitat development and vegetation management.) In Virginia Beach, where Mt. Trashmore required multiple fixes over the decades, the original 1974 capping and the 1986 recapping were paid for by the public works department; the 2003 recapping—hopefully the last—was financed by the park department through its capital improvement budget. In Fresno, California, the landfill isn't even being officially transferred over; the public utilities department will own it in perpetuity but will sign a management agreement with the parks and recreation department.

Frankly, a cheap purchase price is important because preparation costs can be significant. Depending on the age and contents of the landfill, the amount of groundwater or soil contamination, and the planned recreational use, construction costs have ranged from $500,000 for a 2-acre site to $30 million for a regional park of more than 100 acres. Expenses depend on such factors as topography, availability of materials, cover design, and much more. A calculation by the Center for City Park Excellence puts the average at around $300,000 per acre. Financial responsibility for these and other costs may lie solely with the park developer or be shared by the landfill owner/operator.

The construction of municipal solid waste landfills has been regulated since 1991 by the EPA. Today an owner/operator must install a 24-inch earthen cover within six months of closure to minimize water infiltration and erosion. The cover usually also has a gas venting layer and a stone or synthetic biotic layer to keep out burrowing animals.

The EPA requires groundwater monitoring and leachate collection for thirty years after the landfill is closed.

Technically, the two big challenges to using a former landfill are gas production and ground settlement. Landfill gases, including methane, carbon dioxide, ammonia, and hydrogen sulfide, are created when buried waste decomposes. Methane may be released for thirty or more years after closure, and the EPA requires gas collection systems. (In parks built on pre-1991 landfills there were occasional stories of picnickers being stunned to see a column of flame surrounding a barbeque grill.) Happily, methane collected from landfills can be sold by park departments to generate revenue. In Portland, Oregon, St. Johns Landfill, a former disposal site within the 2,000-acre Smith-Bybee Wetlands Natural Area, earns more than $100,000 a year from methane that is piped 2 miles to heat the lime kiln of a cement company. The revenue helps pay for closure operations as the site transitions from landfill to park.

Settlement is a bit tougher. Like cereal in a box, municipal landfills gradually slump as much as 20 percent over a two- or three-decade period. That much settlement would cause foundations to break and sink, utility and irrigation pipes to burst, roads and paths to crack and heave, light poles to tilt, and sports fields to crumple. Obviously, if the ultimate reuse of a landfill is as a natural wildland, none of this matters. But most recreational reuses require the construction of at least trails if not fields and buildings of various types. Fortunately, waste sits only in "cells" in certain areas of a landfill, and park facilities can be safely constructed over undisturbed areas, leaving the settling sections to support grass and shrubbery. Therefore, structural foundations can be protected through detailed research and careful planning; the key is to know exactly where the waste is. At New York's Fresh Kills only about 45 percent of the land area was actually used for waste disposal.

Despite the many successful individual examples, there is not yet a seamless landfills-to-parks movement in the United States. Numerous challenges remain—technological, political, and legal—all of which drive up costs. Back when land was more easily available, the impediments were generally not worth taking on. Now in many cases they are. With a three-pronged effort to design safer waste dumps, to work more closely with community activists, and to ensure protection from legal liabilities, cities will be able to gain much new parkland from abandoned landfills.

CHAPTER 15

Wetlands and Stormwater Storage Ponds

For environmental, financial, and legal reasons, urban stormwater management is getting much more attention. Once, flood-control engineers would prescribe the construction of straight, deep concrete channels, and one stream after the next would be converted into sterile spillways. (The poster channelized waterway, the Los Angeles River, was used for a spine-tingling truck chase scene in the movie *Terminator 2* and was once also proposed—seriously—for use as a highway.) Fortunately, those days are mostly gone. Cities that still have extensive natural wetland areas are carefully protecting them to contain and filter stormwater; many others are now also creating artificial swales and other storage areas to slow down and capture the sheets of water running off streets and asphalt surfaces.

When it comes to water management and recreation, parks as ponds and ponds as parks are two sides of the same coin. The former side doesn't technically add parkland but it makes existing parks more environmentally productive; the latter can add to a city's de facto parkland inventory and, of course, adds a second bin of funding opportunities— all the state and federal water protection programs—to the fundraising arsenal. There is no question that the marriage of stormwater retention and parks will become more common in the coming decades, for both ecological and economic reasons.

New York City, in addition to the thousands of acres under Department of Parks and Recreation control, has another 480 acres of so-called Blue Belt land under the jurisdiction of the Department of Environmental Protection (DEP). The Blue Belt, located largely but not entirely in Staten Island (the least built-up of the city's five boroughs), consists of mapped wetlands that DEP acquires for stormwater management. The Blue Belts are zoned as open space and are protected from development, although the protection is not as stringent as for mapped parkland. Parkland can only be demapped and "alienated" from the park system through a vote of the state legislature; DEP lands can be sold to a private party if the buyer agrees to protect the official drainage corridors that traverse it—no property owner is allowed to modify a watercourse. Although the Blue Belt lands are partially fenced (to help focus the points of ingress and egress), they are fully open to the public. "Since we're spending Water Board money and aren't supposed to be spending it on recreation uses," said Dana Gumb, director of the Staten Island Bluebelt, "we don't specifically build any walking trails or other features. But we do have lightly used maintenance access pathways which we're happy to let people utilize, if they do so appropriately."

The converse occurs when DEP utilizes official park property for water management and water purification. "We'll install a storm sewer system under a street to catch rainwater from a neighborhood, and then we'll daylight it—bring it up to the surface—in a park," said Gumb. "We've done that in Conference House Park, Lemon Creek Park, Wolf's Pond, Bloomingdale Park, and others." The department constructs a pond-like water detention and treatment facility that holds the rainwater for about twenty-four hours, absorbs much of the destructive energy of the rushing torrent, allows sediment to settle out, and then permits the cleaned water to seep gradually into Raritan Bay and the Atlantic Ocean. "We're usually able to locate the holding ponds in areas that had previously been degraded," Gumb explained. "Places that had been disturbed with fill or were overrun with invasive vines. We use the opportunity to fix them up. When we're done the community ends up with something beautiful that also cleans the water."

Although many other municipalities regulate how individuals and commercial entities impact stormwater, almost none currently uses a municipal agency to construct and operate control facilities, and no other city has an agency as sensitive to public recreational use as New York's DEP. Of course, it's not always smooth sailing. There are times when DEP's ecological requirements conflict with the community's desires and the aesthetics of a park. In neighborhoods with combined sewers that mix household wastewater with street stormwater for joint processing, huge underground holding tanks with pumps and smokestacks are required to cope with the influx from large storms. In the worst of those cases the facility can be a blight on a corner of a park. Even in the best cases with successful restoration, a park may be closed for several years during construction.

"There've been instances where DEP has had to pay dearly for the use of parkland," said Gumb. Perhaps most famous was a multiyear battle over the installation of a mammoth underground drinking water storage tank in Van Cortlandt Park in the Bronx. Although the tank was to be completely buried and invisible to park users, the construction project was so large and was slated to take so long that the courts ruled that it was effectively an "alienation" of parkland and would need to be approved by the state legislature. After protracted negotiations, DEP agreed to pay the Parks Department $200 million for the temporary loss of parkland; the money was used to buy and improve dozens of other parks in the Bronx.

As public awareness grows, potentially even more could be done with water detention facilities. In some cases boardwalks, benches, and interpretive signage could be added to these natural and manmade marshy areas to put them to double use for walking, running, and cycling. Some stormwater storage areas could conceivably also be used as dry-weather playing fields or skateboard parks if they are fitted with proper warning signage, fencing, and a commitment to hosing down residue following each high-water incident.

When the Seattle Housing Authority planned the demolition of the distressed High Point public housing site and its transformation into a new mixed-income community, the authority was required to capture all stormwater to keep it from running off the property. The water was required to be released gradually rather than being funneled destructively into a nearby salmon-bearing stream. But when it considered the aesthetics of the standard, unadorned, chain-link-surrounded holding pit, the authority balked. Instead, it created an extensive 130-acre drainage system culminating in one-and-a-quarter-acre Viewpoint Park with benches, a boulder-filled stream, a pond, a trail, a grass lawn, stairs, a playground, and gardens. "We turned what could've been a huge liability into an incredible asset for the community—in a place with a direct view of downtown Seattle," says Tom Phillips, project manager. Constructed by the Housing Authority, the park has been turned over to the Parks and Recreation Department for management and maintenance.

Troutman Park in Fort Collins, Colorado, similarly combines recreational amenities with stormwater management. Designed in 1986 by landscape architecture firm EDAW, the 20-acre park was incorporated into an existing regional water detention basin. The basin consists of an upper pond where sediment settles and a lower pond where water is stored for irrigation. The connecting drainage channel that bisects the site was designed to look like a natural stream, which makes it fun for children and attractive for wildlife. The park's central area includes tennis and basketball courts, a picnic shelter, a playground, and a restroom.

CHAPTER 16

Rail Trails

In 1963 famed Morton Arboretum naturalist May Theilgaard Watts wrote a letter to the editor of the *Chicago Tribune*. "We are human beings," she wrote. "We walk upright on two feet. We need a footpath. Right now there is a chance for Chicago and its suburbs to have a footpath, a long one." Her visionary and poetic letter led to the creation of the Illinois Prairie Path and marked the beginning of the rails-to-trails movement.

Until the interstate highway program in the 1950s, the world's best-engineered rights-of-way were railroad corridors. Hills and cliffs were excavated, valleys filled, curves softened, tunnels dug, and bridges built, all to provide routes of exquisitely smooth gentleness with little or no cross-traffic. They were also extraordinarily well routed from, to, and through the centers of activity—cities. Today, 130,000 miles of these marvelous linear connections have been abandoned. Already, 1,500 segments totaling 15,000 miles have been turned into trails for biking, skiing, skating, running, and walking. Most are rural but the urban ones almost invariably become the spines of city biking networks that also include on-road bike lanes and other feeder-collector routes. Rail trails have become focal points for nonmotorized transportation and recreation in Seattle; Washington, D.C.; Boston; Indianapolis; Dallas; Cincinnati; Spokane; Milwaukee; St. Petersburg; Albany, New York; Arlington, Virginia; Barrington, Rhode Island; and scores of other cities and towns (see table 16.1). And there are still abandoned corridors available for conversion into trails.

Minneapolis shows the multiple types of rail trails and their power to affect a city's park, recreation, and transportation systems. Most dramatic is the Stone Arch Bridge over the Mississippi, built by railroad baron James J. Hill for his Great Northern route to Seattle. Opened in 1883, it was in rail service until 1978. Rescued from demolition,

Table 16.1   Goodbye Train, Hello Trail
Selected Major Urban Rail Trails

Trail	City	Year Opened
Burke-Gilman Trail	Seattle	1978
Burlington Bike Path	Burlington, Vt.	1987
Springwater Trail	Portland, Ore.	1991
Capital Crescent Trail	Washington, D.C.	1994
Stone Arch Bridge	Minneapolis	1994
Three Rivers Trail	Pittsburgh	1996
Monon Trail	Indianapolis	1997
Eastern Promenade Trail	Portland, Me.	1998
Midtown Greenway	Minneapolis	1998
Harrisburg Trail	Houston	2000
Katy Trail	Dallas	2000
Hank Aaron State Trail	Milwaukee	2000
Charlotte Trolley Trail	Charlotte, N.C.	2002
East Boston Greenway	Boston	2003
Orange Line Bikeway	Los Angeles	2005
Columbia Tap Rail Trail	Houston	2009
The High Line	New York	2009
Dequindre Cut Greenway	Detroit	2009

Source: Rails-to-Trails Conservancy

the bridge was refurbished for nonmotorized use through a variety of federal, state, and local funds and ultimately turned over to the Minneapolis Park and Recreation Board. Today it is the keystone of the bicycle/pedestrian network in both Minneapolis and St. Paul. A few blocks away is the Midtown Greenway, created from a former Milwaukee Road track that maintained separation from traffic by being sunk in a box-shaped trench below street level. The 5.5-mile trail today serves several thousand bicyclists, runners, and skaters per day (plus skiers during the long winter); in the future it will also host an extension of the light-rail system on a parallel track in the same trench. The corridor was bought for $10 million by the Hennepin County Regional Railroad Authority. Trail engineering and construction, which cost $25 million, were paid from a variety of local, regional, state, and federal sources. Annual maintenance, which includes lighting and snow plowing, comes to about $500,000 a year.

A couple of miles north, a different set of tracks has been converted into the Cedar Lake Park and Trail. This isn't a rail-*to*-trail, it's a rail-*with*-trail. When the Burlington Northern Railroad decided to divest itself of an underutilized freight yard, it kept one track for through service and sold the rest to the Park Board. The Board erected a fence and converted the wide industrial facility into a model nature habitat with three meandering, parallel treadways—two one-way paths for cyclists and skaters, and one soft-surface path for walkers and runners. With an extraordinary amount of community support, volunteerism, and sweat equity, the 48-acre project cost only $3.5 million to acquire and develop, and it was finished in a record six years.

Six years is a record? Well, yes. Creating a rail trail, candidly, is not easy. The land ownership issues are confusing. Legal and regulatory complexities stretch from the local level to the state capital to Washington, D.C. Railroad companies frequently have unfathomable bureaucracies and are generally uncooperative. Invariably, there is at least one obstreperous adjacent landowner opposed to a trail. While fears about trackside environmental contamination are usually overblown, on occasion toxicity is found and needs rectifying. Many private and public agencies are interested in corridors for roads, transit, and utility lines, and they materialize as competitors. A review of years to complete a trail validates the difficulty: for the Capital Crescent Trail in Washington, D.C., eleven years from conception to ribbon-cutting; for the Pinellas Trail in St. Petersburg, fifteen years; for the Minuteman Trail in Arlington, Massachusetts, eighteen years; for the Metropolitan Branch Trail in Washington, D.C., twenty-two years and (as of this writing) counting.

But the final results justify the heartache: These are truly "million-dollar trails." Other than on a former railroad track, it is simply not possible in an existing built-up community to create a new pathway that is long, straight, wide, continuous, sheathed in vegetation, and almost entirely separated from traffic. And the annual usership numbers reveal the pent-up desire lines: 2 million on the Minuteman Trail outside of Boston; 3 million on the Washington and Old Dominion Trail outside of Washington, D.C.; 1.7 million on the Baltimore and Annapolis Trail; 1.1 million on the East Bay Bicycle Path outside of Providence, Rhode Island; and 1 million on the Capital Crescent Trail in Washington, D.C.

Many park directors initially shy away from taking on the challenge of a rail trail. This is a serious mistake. In addition to all the connectivity and usership values, rail trails often have ecological and historical values very much in keeping with an urban park system's mission. With corridor widths of 60 to 100 feet, or even more in the West, they frequently harbor interesting, unusual, and rare plant species on their margins; in the Midwest, rail lines are often the only remaining places that were never disturbed by the plow and still have original prairie vegetation. Historically they have numerous artifacts, including bridges, tunnels, semaphores, signs, rail spikes, sidings, and frequently also stations, cabooses, and more, available for restoration and interpretation. Moreover, trails are so popular that they have radically increased the support base for virtually every park agency that has ever taken one on.

The reality is that creating one of these trails is so tough that it requires a partnership between a park department (or sometimes a public works or transportation department) and the private sector (usually a citizen group, sometimes a foundation or corporation). The financial and legal issues are too much for a group of volunteers to handle alone, while the political issues are too intense for a government agency without citizen support. In fact, wherever there isn't at least one group of ardent trail lovers—bicyclists, generally—the rail-trail effort usually collapses. Some of these conversions are so difficult that a national organization, the Rails-to-Trails Conservancy, formed specifically to provide technical, legal, financial, and political assistance to communities around the country. The Trust for Public Land is another national organization that has been unusually active with creating urban rail trails, including in Portland, Maine; Boston; Sarasota, Florida; St. Louis; Susanville, California; Chicago; and Tallahassee.

More than that, trail advocates are fierce in their commitment to these facilities—many see them literally as "do or die" opportunities. (More than one, in fact, got started in the grim aftermath of a cyclist's death in a roadway accident.) In Pinellas County, Florida, home to St. Petersburg and Clearwater, when supporters of the Pinellas Trail learned that its construction hinged upon passage of a highly controversial penny-for-infrastructure tax hike, they hurled themselves passionately into the campaign, putting it over the top by 398 votes out of 135,000 cast. (The county administrator called the next day and said, "I'm telling the engineering department tomorrow that the trail project is the first to come out of the chute.") In Seattle, when the *Post-Intelligencer* newspaper reported that the Burlington Northern Railroad had secretly sold off a piece of track that had been slated for a continuation of the Burke-Gilman Trail, cyclists were so outraged that they chained their bikes across the entranceway of Burlington Northern's Seattle head-quarters and began a vehement protest that stayed on the front pages for two months. (The railroad, which had sold the land to an out-of-state tycoon for a place to dock his yacht, found a way to rescind the deal, and the corridor is now the trail extension.) In Washington, D.C., when the National Park Service was unable to get a quick congressional appropriation to save the Georgetown Branch from being developed by CSX Railroad into a string of million-dollar homes through a national park, land developer Kingdon Gould III loaned $12 million of his own money and held the land for a year until Congress acted. (The corridor is today the Capital Crescent Trail, centerpiece of what will eventually be a 20-mile "bicycle beltway" within the nation's capital.)

Even "regular folks" wax poetic over these facilities. When the Seattle Parks and Recreation Department did a survey of Burke-Gilman Trail users in 1986 it was surprised by comments like: "This trail has changed my life," "I would do about anything to support the upkeep and extension of this trail and the promotion of other trails in the city," and "This is the way I'd like to see my taxes used." Hearing that kind of support, the agency has never shied away from a trail project.

The latest innovation is the overhead or trestle trail. Influenced by the creation in Paris, France, of the Promenade Plantée ("Planted Walk-way"), activists in New York, Chicago, and St. Louis have all discovered abandoned rail trestles and launched campaigns to bring them back as trails. First to open, in 2009, was New York's High Line, a sensa-tional tour de force in the now-chic former meatpacking district. The walkway (which from day one was so crowded with pedestrians that bicycles were not permitted) includes sophisticated plantings, architec-tural landscaping reminiscent of railroad tracks, artistic benches and chaise lounges, a viewing gallery with picture window overlooking 10th Avenue traffic, a large wall of glass panes dyed every hue of the Hudson River, food carts, seating areas, and more.

A bit less upscale but considerably longer and designed for cy-clists as well as walkers, Chicago's Bloomingdale Trail is expected to open in segments as funds for the $45-million conversion are found. The Bloomingdale Trail should serve recreational cyclists as well as purposeful commuters since one day it could join an interconnected trailway linking Lake Michigan to the Mississippi River. St. Louis's Iron Horse Trestle will also prove helpful to cyclists, runners, and walkers of all stripes since it passes over busy Interstate 70 and leads toward the popular Riverfront Trail along the Mississippi River.

CHAPTER 17

Rooftops

New York landscape architect Thomas Balsley delights in promising to show friends what he calls "the greatest untapped open space opportunity in America." He then takes them to the top of the Empire State Building and points to the ocean of rooftops visible to the horizon in every direction.

A city receives exactly as much sunlight and rainfall as it did before development when the area was a virgin forest or grassland, but now much of the meteorological action is off the ground on top of structures. Although most individual houses have sloping roofs that are perhaps better suited for solar collectors or conduits for rain barrels, most large institutional or residential buildings have flat ones that could potentially be used for parks. Rooftops represent the rare resource that is increasing. Most are private, but a significant number are publicly owned. And some of those are large—the tops of schools, libraries, government office buildings, post offices, concert halls, convention centers, parking ramps, and bus stations can all extend to well over an acre. Moreover, large private rooftops, such as those on shopping centers, big-box stores, and warehouses, are purchasable or leasable, just like any other private property.

The green roof movement, still in its infancy, is mushrooming in popularity along with the green building movement in general. Even the Wal-Mart Corporation is experimenting with a colossal green roof on a store in Chicago. But merely being green does not make a roof a park—there are hundreds of planted roofs but barely a handful of them are official parks. The primary driving factors for the planted roof are ecological and economic—making a building perform better so that it saves energy, conserves water, and reduces costs. (To prove that point, researchers took a thermometer up to the roof of the City-County Building in Chicago on a bright, sunny, 70-degree day. They found that the temperature on the Chicago City Hall side of the edifice, which is famously covered with soil and planted, was 74 degrees; on the unimproved Cook County side it was 151 degrees.) On the other hand, the primary driving factors for the rooftop park is recreational—squeezing out of the cramped city a bit more space with sun and air for public enjoyment.

That oft-cited Chicago City Hall green roof is a marvelous creation but it isn't a park, just as the much older green roof on the Time-Life Building in New York City isn't a park—neither is freely open to the public. There are already thousands of rooftop gardens, pools, and recreational facilities on top of luxury condominiums, apartment buildings, office buildings, and hotels across the country, but they are private facilities for residents, workers, guests, and members only. They are the vertical equivalent of parks inside gated communities. Although they have great value to users and even some benefit to nonusers (by providing a smidgeon of wildlife habitat and taking a bit of pressure off public parks), they should not be counted in any citywide park inventory, just as country clubs aren't counted.

At present the majority of rooftop parks are ones at ground level built over subsurface parking garages—places like Millennium Park in Chicago, Hudlin Park in St. Louis, and Yerba Buena Garden in San Francisco. This wonderful urban solution is referred to, at Boston's Post Office Square, as "Park Above, Park Below." Older facilities are of relatively conventional ornamental design; new ones increasingly incorporate more ecological features. Both Nashville's new Public Square and Austin's new City Hall collect all the gathered rain for later use as pumped irrigation water. (In Austin, the majority of the roof is at ground level over a subsurface parking garage, but parts of it climb up the building itself as a series of park-like balconies.)

Putting parks on rooftops higher than street level is, thus far, much rarer. For one thing, keeping the plant material alive is a challenge because of more extreme conditions of wind, sunlight, thin soil, and lack of trees. For another, there are concerns about the structural strength of buildings and potential water leakage as well as issues of human access and security. Also, what park uses are appropriate on rooftops? Flower gardens, lawns, benches, and pathways? Courts (surrounded by cages) for basketball, tennis, and volleyball? Community gardens? Playgrounds? Dog parks? Miniature golf?

These are complex questions that require a good deal of research—both into the issue of "rooftops" and of "parks." Some of the investigation is generic, some of it needs to be highly specific, on a city-by-city basis. How many flat rooftops does, say, Miami have? What is the total combined acreage? How many are on public buildings and what is that combined acreage? How many of them are large, say, an acre or more? How many of those large ones are relatively uncluttered with air conditioning units and other paraphernalia? How many are accessible by the public? How many happen to be in areas underserved by parks? This entire field of inquiry is so new that there are almost no data available, although there will be breathtakingly quick progress now that aerial photography is so widely available through Internet programs.

One of the most famous, and one of the oldest, rooftop parks is NCNB Plaza (also called Kiley Garden) in Tampa, Florida. Rarely known for urban innovation, Tampa backed into its moment of leadership as a result of authentic civic outrage over the sale and destruction of its historic rose garden for the erection of a 33-story bank tower. In a creative (and expensive) gesture of repair, North Carolina National Bank agreed to restore the lost green space by putting a park on top of the new tower's parking deck. Designed by (and named after) prominent landscape architect Dan Kiley and opened in 1988, the plaza is 8 feet above ground level. It is a highly geometric and stylized park with severe architectural elements on a mathematical grid that provoked strong outpourings of both praise and criticism when it was unveiled. While a celebrated space, it was never hugely popular, either because of its cold design or its out-of-view location, or because downtown Tampa is still decidedly a nine-to-five, Monday-to-Friday neighborhood.

Kiley Garden represents all that is great and all that is problematical about rooftop parks. On the positive side, it provides outstanding views of Tampa's downtown and of the Hillsborough River and its riverwalk. It came into being in a high-land-value location that, under other circumstances, would never have yielded a public park. On the other hand, there were design and construction shortcomings that ultimately—nineteen years later—forced a total and complete renovation, including the removal of every tree, shrub, and blade of grass, as well as the many architectural elements. Of course, almost every aspect of technology has evolved in the past two decades, and the lessons of

Kiley Garden can be used to help make rooftop parks more successful in the future.

A new green roof in Denver comes very close to being a park although, ironically, it doesn't allow users "on the grass" (not that there is anything as mundane there as grass). It's located on the roof of the Denver Botanic Garden's café and gift shop, and the 2,000-square-foot space showcases fifty different native and drought-tolerant plants, including beard tongue, penstemon, ice plant, prickly pear cactus, hedgehog cactus, and Bell's bladder pod. The space is given more than three-quarters to plants and one-quarter for visitors to enjoy them, with a stone knee wall separating them. It was constructed for only $60,000 on the top of an exceptionally strong roof. "Fortunately the building was designed in the 1960s when concrete was all the rage, and it's built like a bunker," said Senior Horticulturist Mark Fusco. The purpose of the project is not primarily to provide more green space to the Botanic Garden's visitors (who, after all, already bask in a large and beautiful park-like setting at ground level) but to demonstrate the many possibilities of green roofs and to test the rooftop hardiness of different species. In its literature and tours the Botanic Garden emphasizes that green roofs can reduce heating and cooling costs; extend the lifespan of the roofing membrane by protecting it from ultraviolet rays and temperature changes; increase habitat for birds, insects, and wildlife; and reduce noise. As these advantages become known throughout society, architects, developers, and government building agency staffs may give more consideration to full-fledged rooftop parks. Similarly, mayors, planning commissions, and city zoning boards might begin encouraging, requiring, or giving bonuses for rooftop parks on redevelopment projects in dense, park-poor neighborhoods.

The two places that have taken rooftop parks the furthest are New York and San Francisco—not surprisingly, since they are the two most crowded cities in the country. New York can boast of the largest rooftop park, but San Francisco can counter with the most imaginative piece of legislation to promote these new facilities.

At 28 acres, New York's Riverbank State Park is so large that it contains a pool, a skating rink, a theater, four tennis courts, four basketball courts, a wading pool, a softball field, a football field, four handball courts, a running track, two playgrounds, a weight room, a boat dock, and a restaurant. It was built on the roof of a new sewage treatment plant on the Hudson River and provides an exciting template of how large public buildings can be constructed to do double duty.

As for San Francisco, not only does it have by-now-somewhat-traditional rooftop parks above underground parking garages at Union Square, Portsmouth Square, and a part of Golden Gate Park, but it also has St. Mary's Square, a full-fledged, off-the-ground, up-in-the-air park amid the high rises in the Financial District. Moreover, St. Mary's Square will soon be getting an addition (on another rooftop) thanks to a far-reaching law—Proposition K, the Sunlight Ordinance—passed by voters in 1989. That ordinance, aimed at preventing the proliferation of shadows in already-chilly San Francisco, restricts any new construction that would block sunlight on a public park. (Among other things, the law gave birth to a unit of measurement that has probably never existed anywhere else in history: the "solar-year square-foot-hour of new shade.") St. Mary's is the place where the irresistible force of San Francisco's development pressure met the immovable object of the arc of solar radiation.

Because of its location and open-space importance to workers and residents, St. Mary's was given the most stringent designation under Proposition K: zero tolerance. The square could not have a single additional square-foot-hour of sunlight taken away. An office tower was proposed that would have blocked a small amount of sunlight—only in the early morning, four months out of the year—but that was enough to kill the proposal, until a wonderful solution was proposed. The developer offered to create a public park on the second-floor roof of the building's garage. The 5,000-square-foot roof was located in such a way that it received much more sunlight; in fact, the developer calculated that the amount of sunlight hitting the rooftop park addition would be 40 times greater than the sunlight lost to the old park by the building's shadow. And, because of the steepness of the site, the second-story location actually intersected with the ground plane of a portion of St. Mary's Square, removing the need for steps or handicap accessible designs. It is fitting that San Francisco would be the site of a new kind of political math: Ridiculously Stringent Law plus Exorbitantly Expensive Real Estate equals Unprecedented New Kind of Park.

Overcoming the hurdles of rooftop park technology and getting people up off the ground can be challenging. But rooftop parks could make a big difference when it comes to urban beauty, livability, and recreation. This abundant resource beckons, particularly in extremely dense communities that are very short of parkland—places like Brooklyn, Miami, lower Manhattan, Chicago's near west side, South Los Angeles, and, of course, San Francisco's financial district. (See appendix 1 for citywide density comparisons.)

CHAPTER 18

Sharing Schoolyards

Schoolyards are large, flat, centrally located open spaces with a mandate to serve the recreational needs of schoolchildren. Great schoolyards—the rare ones that have healthy grass, big trees, a playground, and sports equipment—seem a lot like parks. But they aren't. For one thing, most have fences and locks. For another, they are closed to the general public. Schoolyards are parks for only a limited constituency. But they have terrific potential to be more than that. Even less-than-great schoolyards (those that are merely expanses of asphalt with few amenities) represent sizable opportunities in key locations. To many observers, schoolyards seem the best, most obvious source of park-like land to supplement the park systems of overcrowded cities. And they are—even if upgrading them into schoolyard parks is more difficult than it might seem.

"Schoolyard park" in this context means a space reserved for schoolchildren during school hours and used by the whole community at other times. In a few cities—New York, Chicago, and Phoenix—schoolyard parks are run cooperatively by the board of education and the parks department. In others, the parks department has no formal role at all.

Creating a multiagency urban schoolyard park program requires attention to detail, clarity of authority, and ongoing acceptance of responsibility. Most of all it requires unflinching commitment to success, which is why the arrangement succeeds more frequently when the school system and the park system are both under the control of the mayor. Without that kind of singular authority, one or the other bureaucracy can simply bolt from an agreement if an obstacle arises.

Challenges number one and two relate to surfacing and maintenance. Most schoolyards originally had grass and trees. But without proper design, construction, and maintenance, grass can't survive daily trampling by hundreds of little feet. And small trees can't handle that much swinging and climbing without becoming spindly skeletons.

After a few years of frustration with dust, mud, and dead trees, school principals begin to think that laying down asphalt might be a superior solution (and barely any worse ecologically). It's also a lot easier to sweep up broken glass from asphalt than from dirt and weeds. Then, this being America, the expanse of asphalt starts to attract automobiles; in no time the former school park has a set of parallel white lines and a row of oil stains. Keeping a schoolyard green, clean, car-free, and environmentally productive can be more difficult than operating a regular neighborhood park.

Maintenance can also be thorny. Most school districts are either unable or unwilling to keep schoolyards up to the standards that parks require. After all, money spent on horticulture for the community at large is money not spent on the education of children. But school districts also generally balk at turning the maintenance responsibility over to the park department. They worry about losing control over their children's space.

There are successful programs to refurbish school lands in both Boston (the Boston Schoolyard Initiative) and Denver (Learning Land scapes). Both programs are fully under the direction and control of the school system with no involvement of the park department. The schoolyards are open to the general community except during school hours; they are all fenced. Converting each former space in Denver from what one administrator called "scorched earth that resembled a prison yard" into an irrigated and drained Learning Landscape with a field, two play structures, a hard-surface court, and a "community gateway" (an archway that invites the public both symbolically and physically) costs about $450,000. Boston schoolyards, which at about a quarter of an acre are considerably smaller, cost about $320,000 each for a new drainage system, plantings, hard-surface area, play equipment, fences, decorative art, and an "outdoor classroom" with a micro-meadow, -woodland, and -garden. As with so many other innovative ideas about the use of urban space, conflicts have arisen about cars. At one Boston site, a bitter battle broke out when some parents proposed converting a school parking lot into a soccer field; ultimately the soccer moms raised $200,000 in private funds and got their way.

Another successful program is Spark (School Park Program) in Houston, where the facilities are called Spark Parks. The program is run by a nonprofit in close cooperation with the mayor's office. It works only with Houston-area school boards, not with any park department, but it has a strict requirement that the public must have access to the Spark parks after school hours and on weekends. The average Spark park costs between $75,000 and $100,000 and consists of modular play equipment, picnic tables, benches, an outdoor classroom (concrete steps and stage), a butterfly garden, a paved or crushed granite trail, and native trees. Founded in 1983, Spark created 203 parks in its first 25 years. In affluent neighborhoods, funds are procured from county commissioners, philanthropists, and corporations; in needier areas, money is apportioned by the mayor through his federal Community Development Block Grant allotment; in every case, the school itself is required to contribute $5,000, which is raised via bake sales, penny drives, rummage sales, and other events. Since 1990 the Spark program has put special emphasis on artwork, often murals or mosaics that the children help with. "It has become extremely popular," said Spark Director Kathleen Ownby. "We've become one of the largest providers of outdoor art in the Houston area."

Challenge number three relates to joint use. The primary users of schoolyards are schoolchildren whose needs predominate. The time division is often something like dawn to 8 a.m. for community use, 8 a.m. to 3 p.m. for school uses, and then 3 p.m. to dark plus weekends for community use again. Because of the children, schoolyards are generally locked during school hours. While theoretically a minor issue, locks can cause unending problems, particularly if there is no park attendant or custodian on the premises. The central issue is: Who's in charge? If the school system, the grounds are likely to be more tightly monitored but not as well maintained. If the park department controls and if the schoolyard is truly open as a neighborhood space, upkeep may be better but oversight of the children might be slightly compromised—there have been complaints of young early-morning users sometimes finding drug and sex paraphernalia in school parks that were open to the community the night before. (Others claim that the increased community use makes them safer than if they are locked.) The community is always enthusiastic about a daytime play-park for children, mothers, and families to get exercise, open space, and sociability. But there is usually less enthusiasm about nighttime use with its noise and questionable activities. In some cases, the neighborhood decides to install only one hoop for basketball rather than a full court because a half-court makes

for a less attractive facility. Even so, schoolyard park fences are periodically scaled or cut, as with school properties everywhere, and must be
repaired.

Many joint-use agreements break down over what *seems* to be an issue of legal liability but in fact is a smokescreen for more subjective factors of personality, power, and control. In Houston, the liability issue
was resolved when the state of Texas agreed to indemnify schools and
cities from certain incidents that occur on public grounds (aside from
those due to inadequate maintenance). But in Philadelphia agreement
over liability was never reached because there was no higher authority
to force deadlocked negotiations to continue. (Until 2009, neither the
Board of Education nor the Fairmount Park Commission was under
the control of the mayor.)

Chicago and New York are among the few cities where, because of
mayoral interest, a partnership operates successfully between the board
of education and the department of parks. In Chicago, in 1996, Mayor
Richard M. Daley, following a successful pilot program, announced
an ambitious goal of converting 100 asphalt schoolyards into small
parks. Called the Campus Park Program, it involved the creation of
playgrounds, baseball fields, basketball and tennis courts, and running
tracks on a total of 150 acres. It was completed four years later at a cost
of $43 million—$20 million each from the school system and the city,
plus $3 million from the park district. Design was handled by the park
district and construction by the Public Buildings Commission, and the
process was guided by way of meetings among park and school officials, principals, local school councils, and community organizations.
Ongoing maintenance is handled largely by the school district with as-
needed assistance from the park district for larger properties and more
park-deficient neighborhoods.

New York City has taken the concept the furthest. There, with
the blessing of Mayor Michael Bloomberg, the Trust for Public Land
(TPL) entered into a partnership with the Department of Education,
the Department of Parks and Recreation, and private funders (including MetLife, Credit Suisse, Deutsche Bank, and The Michael and
Susan Dell Foundation) to convert scores of decrepit and uninviting
schoolyards into showcase parks. The program is simple in concept,
complex in practice, and diverse in implementation. The school recreation grounds are owned by the Department of Education, but the

renovation work is overseen by the Department of Parks and TPL. Though the mayor is technically in control, New York does not have a political culture where "thou shalt" decrees are sent from headquarters. Many decisions are made by the principal, the parent-teacher association, and the community. Proposals can be killed by teachers who don't want to lose parking spaces, by custodians who don't want to handle park maintenance, or by communities that don't want kids out late playing basketball.

"This program is community-run," says Mary Alice Lee, director of TPL's New York City Playground Program. While all properties are fenced and have locks, in some places it's the school custodial staff that has the only key, while in others it's held by the neighborhood sponsoring organization or a block association. A few of the parks are left permanently unlocked. Also, each community sets its own hours. Most common is a schedule of 8 a.m. to dusk seven days a week except when school is in session. In some tougher neighborhoods the community wants the park closed earlier; the most restrictive schedule is 3 p.m. to 6 p.m. weekdays, 10 a.m. to 2 p.m. Saturdays, and closed on Sundays.

Designing the space itself is a delicate balancing act that can take up to three months. The children themselves are the lead designers, responding to a set of questions and opportunities posed by TPL, but of course there are a bevy of realities that also affect decisions, including liability, equipment breakability, horticultural survivability, cost, and life lessons from previous play-parks. The children work hard, learning how to innovate, compromise, and reach a consensus when their initial ideas turn out to be too expensive or require too much space.

"Because of the kids," says Lee, "we've created murals and mosaics, a hair-braiding area, a jump-rope zone, planting gardens, performance stages, outdoor classrooms, rain gardens, and bowling lanes—as well as the usual soccer fields, running tracks, basketball and tennis courts, and play equipment."

Maintenance is the responsibility of the school custodial staff, so it is important to involve them in all design decisions right from the beginning. Often they turn down a particular piece of equipment; in some cases they have nixed the playground entirely. As for natural grass, it has proven impossible to maintain under intense usage, and TPL now uses only artificial turf for the play-parks' ballfields. Houston's Spark program, in contrast, forbids artificial turf and uses only natural grass.

Whether schoolyard parks have indigenous staying power remains an open question; the movement is young and, in most cities, still operating on the founders' enthusiasm. As with every other new park approach, schoolyard parks entail new levels of effort, money, and commitment. (For the New York TPL project, which added 265 acres of parkland, each play-park, from predesign to ribbon-cutting, cost from $400,000 to $1.2 million, and the full three-year program clocked in at just over $100 million.)

Early evidence suggests that these parks need oversight and advocacy from private friends organizations, either school by school or citywide. Without that kind of support, the numerous "regular" pressures tend to pull school and park officials back to basics and away from this kind of multifaceted experiment. According to TPL's Lee, the private organization can be an after-school group, a robust parent-teacher association, or any other institution that reaches beyond the normal school structure.

CHAPTER 19

Covering Reservoirs

Open drinking water reservoirs have been a fact of urban life, and often-beloved icons, in the United States for well over a century. Highland Park Reservoir (1879), McMillan Reservoir (1903), and Silver Lake Reservoir (1907), among others, were *the* places to promenade, picnic, see, and be seen in Pittsburgh, Washington, D.C., and Los Angeles, respectively. Some, like Baltimore's Druid Hill Park Reservoir, were located within larger park spaces; others, like Compton Hill Reservoir in St. Louis, essentially filled the entire space of their own park-like setting. It was recognized that none of them was entirely hygienic. They were fenced but, after all, at the mercy of general city dust and grime, not to mention bird droppings. But, like Ivory soap in the old commercial, 99.44 percent pure was considered good enough. There are also numerous reservoirs that are not fenced. These reservoirs contain what is called "raw" water that is relatively clean but not yet "finished" for human consumption. At Griggs Reservoir Park in Columbus, Ohio, or White Rock Lake Park in Dallas visitors can go right to the water's edge and dip their toes in, if they wish, or even go boating.

Then in 1993 came a highly publicized outbreak of *cryptosporidium* bacteria in the Milwaukee water supply and, soon after, heightened concerns about terrorism. Attention to public health was raised a notch. In December 2005, after years of deliberation, the U.S. Environmental Protection Agency published something called the Long Term 2 Enhanced Surface Water Rule that mandated that all newly constructed "finished water" reservoirs be built with a cover. (Finished water is clean enough for delivery to homes; raw water still needs treatment before it's drinkable.) As for already-existing finished water reservoirs, the EPA gave municipalities the choice of covering them or leaving them as is and then retreating the water to finish it.

The requirement was greeted with dismay by many people who delight in the view of the open water, but the presence of a cover opens up the possibility for gaining parkland. Seattle, in particular, has recognized this chance to close a park gap in some neighborhoods. In fact, the city (along with the whole state of Washington) got started more than a decade ahead of the EPA rule. As former Mayor Greg Nickels put it, "This is a rare opportunity to turn public works into public parks. Underground reservoirs will not only improve the quality and security of our water supply, they will add to the quality of life in our neighborhoods." All in all, the city is set to add 76 acres of new park land using reservoir decks—including 4 acres in densely populated Capitol Hill, 20 acres in Jefferson Park (with a running track, sports fields, picnic grounds and a large, unprogrammed lawn), and a completely new park on top of Myrtle Reservoir. The $161-million cost is being funded via a rise in residential water use fees.

Wilmington, Delaware, is getting a significant parkland boost from a similar program. Cool Spring Reservoir, which dates to 1875 and is located in a densely populated section, was buried in 2009, adding about 7 acres of parkland to the adjoining 12.5-acre Cool Spring Park. In one swoop, this conversion increased the small city's total parkland resource by 1.6 percent. The expanded park serves about 11,500 residents within a half mile radius.

Under the EPA's rule, cities have the option of covering their finished-water reservoirs with a variety of materials, from air-supported fabric to floating polypropylene, from a dome of aluminum to a flat surface of wood, steel, or concrete. An analysis of possibilities for 15-acre Elysian Reservoir by the Los Angeles Department of Water and Power pegged the cost of a floating cover at $19.6 million, a lightweight aluminum roof at $38.1 million, and a buried concrete tank at $121.4 million. Seattle, of course, found the same type of steep costs, but the mayor's office there conducted a study that showed acquiring a similar amount of other parkland would cost about 85 percent as much as putting the reservoirs in concrete tanks. Michael Shiosaki, Seattle's deputy director of planning said, "There's no way we'd be able to buy properties like this, situated as they are on scenic overlooks in densely built-out locations throughout the city." The concrete decks are covered with 8 inches to 2 feet of soil and planted with grass. They are principally used as open lawn areas, active sports fields, and game courts, interwoven with pathways. Trees are restricted to the perimeter because of the risk of root penetration of the deck.

The tension of shimmering views versus safe drinking water is not new and it's not unsolvable. St. Louis long ago figured out how to do it: For more than 100 years, Compton Hill Reservoir has been covered, but the top of the cover is bowl-shaped and filled with water—nondrinking water—to make for a beautiful park experience. Seattle did something similar, building a small nondrinking water pond and fountain on top of its new Cal Anderson Park deck to memorialize the former reservoir. Wilmington also responded to a neighborhood outcry, putting its reservoir under just half the property and redesigning the other half as a pond with a viewing platform.

Other old reservoirs have been decommissioned and thus represent prime possible sites for parks. In densely populated Jersey City, New Jersey, 13-acre Reservoir #3 is located on a high bluff. Built in 1874 and used for more than a century, it was finally abandoned in the 1970s and became a dumping ground and a camping area for the homeless, its walls and buildings left to deteriorate. The city proposed filling in the site for housing, but residents, who had started to use the reservoir for fishing, kayaking, bird watching, and walking, protested. Finally, a campaign led by the Jersey City Reservoir Preservation Alliance resulted in a commitment by Mayor Jerramiah Healy in February 2007 to turn the land into an official park. The deal was consummated using funding from the city, Hudson County, the state of New Jersey, and several private sources.

Not all reservoir stories have happy outcomes. Washington, D.C.'s McMillan Reservoir, built in the early 1900s and envisioned as a central feature in the city's open space network, has been closed to the public since World War II. The grounds of the reservoir and its associated sand filtration site total 118 acres in a part of the city with little other usable parkland. Originally designed in 1907 by Frederick Law Olmsted, Jr., as a public park with promenades and places for people to sit, the facility is today encircled by a rusty chain-link fence set far back from the water pool itself, precluding any human use of the grounds. Ironically, since the water is unfinished the EPA rule does not come into play and there is no mandate to cover or bury it. The managing agency, the U.S. Army Corps of Engineers, is concerned about possible water contamination and has no plans to remove or move the fence to get better use of the surrounding green space, and the neighborhood is not powerful or well-organized enough to push the Corps to think more creatively.

CHAPTER 20

River and Stream Corridors

Every city has streams, and streamside areas offer some of the most attractive sites for parks. But streams also present flooding hazards, and many have been placed in pipes and sunk underground. Most urban streams that are visible (that is, flowing on the surface) are already within parkland. Often this parkland is narrow and not usable for much other than a trail. In many cases it would be desirable to acquire more land alongside the corridor for a wider ecological and recreational buffer, but that often involves buying and removing houses or other buildings, which is expensive and politically difficult. Sometimes a severe flood offers the municipality the opportunity to acquire and demolish badly damaged structures. The greenway through the center of Rapid City, South Dakota, was created when the city resolved to never rebuild in the flood zone after a catastrophic deluge there in 1972. In Tulsa, following the deadly Memorial Day flood of 1984, 528 creekside houses and mobile homes were purchased and removed and a greenway was constructed with soccer fields, tennis courts, trails, and fishing spots. More recently, the Greater Grand Forks Greenway was created when the Red River floodplain was cleared of structures after the devastating flood in Grand Forks, North Dakota, and East Grand Forks, Minnesota, in 1997. The greenway park totals 2,200 acres and includes a campground, two golf courses, a disc golf course, fishing sites, and 20 miles of multipurpose trails.

In Houston, the Harris County Flood Control District buys large amounts of land alongside bayous (creeks) in order to provide space for water retention and a buffer for flooding. Today, it has jurisdiction over an amazing 2,500 miles of channels. While the District does not initiate trail projects or manage human use, it is more than willing to partner with other government agencies or even citizen organizations in providing for recreation; its best-known trail, along Bray's Bayou, serves hundreds of thousands of cyclists and walkers each year. The Flood Control District receives dedicated tax revenue from all Houston area property owners; however, this is not the only conceivable way to pay for streamside land acquisition. Another possibility would be to upzone the neighborhoods on either side of the widened waterway, allowing for greater density, greater height, more dwelling units, and more property tax revenue—using the bayou park to offer more people pretty views and nearby recreation and to become the seed of new higher-value development.

One place that has focused a great deal of analysis, attention, and money on streams is Mecklenburg County, North Carolina, the county that includes Charlotte. Like Harris County, Mecklenburg buys up vacant, high-flood-risk creekside properties. It is also perfectly willing—anxious, even—to buy at-risk houses and commercial structures, tear them down, and turn the resulting land into greenway parks. This program is a truly gritty one—not just looking at buying virgin land to avoid future flooding costs, but also looking to fix existing inappropriate development problems from the 1940s, 1950s, and 1960s. "The best way to totally eliminate the flooding risk is to remove the structures," says Dave Canaan, the county's director of water and land resources. "I want a situation where we'll never have to dispatch our Swift Water Rescue Team." As of mid-2009, a total of about 120 acres had been purchased in greater Charlotte and 248 structures torn down—most of them after having been flooded numerous times. (These are all "willing buyer–willing seller" situations; in one case, a creekside warehouse owner spurned a buyout offer only to return, hat in hand, after having been catastrophically flooded twice in the following two years.)

In fact, it appears that Mecklenburg County's streamside park program will be expanding in size. In a 1997 deluge, when seventeen properties that were deemed unfloodable flooded, planners realized that something was wrong with their maps. It turned out that they were out of date and didn't take into account increased runoff from all the new development. Relying on the maps was like buying a child a child-sized bed and expecting it to last his lifetime. To make sure that never happened again, Mecklenburg used computer mapping to project "ultimate runoff"—that time in the future when the county is developed to the maximum extent under existing law. The result was dramatic. The 100-year flood stage on the average creek jumped up 4 vertical feet—which widened the average floodplain by 180 feet (to 610 feet rather than the previous 430). This is now the standard the county uses in preventing development or buying at-risk properties.

Not all streamside land immediately becomes parkland—in many cases the Stormwater Services Department needs to first undertake significant hydraulic and erosion control work on the streams. But most of the floodplain eventually gets turned over to Mecklenburg County Parks and Recreation Department. Most impressive of the many projects involves Little Sugar Creek, which runs from a point northeast of center city all the way to the South Carolina border. While portions of the corridor are still in relatively pristine, undeveloped areas, the middle stretch is Charlotte's most urbanized and brutalized waterway. Not only had it been straightened and paved, but significant portions had literally been covered by parking lots for strip developments. (The stream also smelled so bad that in the early twentieth century the city hung casks of perfume under its bridges.) On a regular basis the creek had retaliated against the mistreatment with increasingly costly floods. Finally, in the early 1990s, Charlotte's attitude went through a sea change. No longer would the goal be to move the largest quantity of water as quickly as possible through a concrete-and-culvert channel. Instead, natural processes like sediment-reducing meanders would be reintroduced and the floodplain would be widened and reestablished to give high water a place to go, to slow down, to be temporarily held, and to be gradually released. Scores of houses and commercial buildings were purchased and torn down, large areas of asphalt parking were dug up, the stream was dechanneled, wetlands were established, and a bicycle trail was constructed. In the less built-up stretches, developers are now forbidden from any new construction in the floodway. The long-term goal is not only the rejuvenation of a maligned stream but also the creation of a 15-mile greenway park and trail traversing half the length of Mecklenburg County. (As of 2009, 3.6 miles were open to the public and 2.2 more were under construction.)

Similarly impressive is the way Mecklenburg County funds the project. About half the money comes from park bonds, the other half from stormwater fees paid by every landowner in the county. Interestingly, the fees are set on a sliding scale based on what percentage of a property is impervious. The more a property is covered by a dwelling or paved for other uses—in other words, the more rainwater will run off, contributing to floods—the more the landowner pays. In 2009, a Charlotte residential property owner with less than 2,000 square feet of impervious surface paid $5.83 a month; someone with 5,000 or more square feet of impervious ground paid $10.01 a month. (Using analysis of aerial photography, the Stormwater Services Department literally knows the amount of impervious area on each of the 330,000 improved properties in the county, including the 225,000 residential parcels.) All in all, Mecklenburg County and its fast-growing city of Charlotte have created a well-rounded system for saving stream corridors, using them as greenway parks, reducing flood damages and costs, and establishing a fair and publicly accepted method for paying for the program.

Some visible creeks are not in parks but merely run alongside roads. Occasionally it may be possible to decommission and depave one of these roads, convert it into a walking trail or bikeway, and reclassify the streamside land into parkland. When the city of Baltimore created the Gwynns Falls Trail, part of the route used a former road bordering the stream. Some of the road segments had been damaged in storms while others had been so lightly used they were deemed expendable. The intact portions were left alone and simply reclassified as closed to cars; the wrecked portions were narrowed and rebuilt to look like a traditional trailway.

"Daylighting" buried streams—bringing them back to the surface—is an appealing concept since water adds so much to a park. But the challenges of daylighting should not be minimized. Urban streams were buried so that structures could be built closer to floodplains; except for the pipe it is now inevitable that they would flood those structures. The expense of daylighting stems not so much from removing the pipe but from widening and regrading the bed and the floodplain to prevent siltation, erosion, gouging, and the other problems endemic to streams in altered environments. The hydrology and ecology of even a small stream valley is awesomely complex. In the 1980s, St. Paul, Minnesota, wanted to daylight Phalen Creek though Swede Hollow Park. When water volumes and the confined topography proved too difficult, however, the engineers settled on bringing a portion of the flow to the surface while leaving most of it underground in the pipe. In neighboring Minneapolis, when the city wanted to raise up Bassett Creek through a new park, preventing flooding proved impossible; the city had to settle for the less ecologically "real" solution of digging an artificial stormwater pond in the middle of the park and leaving Basset Creek where it was—underground.

One of the few unmitigated daylighting success stories occurred in the mid-1980s in Berkeley, California, where a citizen group named Urban Ecology lobbied the city to bring Strawberry Creek to the surface. After a lengthy political effort and the appropriation of $580,000, a 200-feet section of creek was daylighted through a park that had been created out of an abandoned rail yard.

The rejuvenation of industrialized urban areas can be expensive, incremental, and slow.

CHAPTER 21

Cemeteries

In the past, before official parks came into being, cemeteries were the principal manicured greenspaces for cities—most famously Mount Auburn Cemetery in Cambridge, Massachusetts, and Greenwood Cemetery in Brooklyn, New York. As parks arose, the recreational use of the open areas of cemeteries diminished in importance. But today some cities have hundreds or thousands of acres of public cemetery lands, both with and without gravestones, which could theoretically help with the parkland shortage. While the most enthusiastic nature lovers tend to regard cemeteries as "of course" parkland, the average urban dweller isn't so sure. Interestingly, the few economic studies of cemetery proximity show that they neither raise nor lower nearby property values—the number of people who would love to live near their calm beauty seems to be balanced by the number who find them upsetting. There are some cemeteries surrounded by high-value, high-density neighborhoods, such as Graceland and Oak Wood Cemeteries in Chicago, but others are barricaded by undesirable uses, like Calvary Cemetery in Queens, New York, encircled by industry, railroad tracks, the Long Island Expressway, and the Brooklyn-Queens Expressway.

Is a cemetery a park? It certainly qualifies as pervious ground and visual relief, but whether it does any more than that depends on its rules and regulations. The more one can do there—walk, walk a dog, cycle, picnic, play music, throw a ball, sit under a tree (does it have trees?)—the more it's like a park. The more restrictive, the less justifiable it seems to pretend it's a park.

The Washington, D.C., area has extremes on either end of this spectrum. At Arlington National Cemetery, which is a vast space almost as large as the entire park system of Arlington, Virginia, virtually nothing is permitted other than walking from grave to grave. Jogging and eating are prohibited and there are almost no benches. Across town, at

venerable (but little-known) Congressional Cemetery, not only is picnicking and child-play allowed but the facility is also a formal off-leash
dog park. (Membership for dog owners is limited to a sustainable number and costs nearly $200 a year, with the funds used to support the
nonprofit organization whose mission is to operate, develop, maintain,
preserve, and enhance the cemetery grounds; use by humans without
dogs is free and unrestricted.)

Another famous cemetery, Cedar Hill in Hartford, Connecticut, not
only allows residents to run, walk dogs, and ride bicycles, but also programs the space with jazz concerts and other events and even allows residents to bring food and wine. In Fort Collins, Colorado, Grand View
Cemetery has the city's finest remaining collection of elm trees and thus
garners a steady stream of birdwatchers. Its dirt roadway system not
only attracts fat-tire cyclists but is also used as a training site by Colorado State University's cross-country team. And in Charleston, West
Virginia, the city-owned Spring Hill Cemetery was formally renamed
Spring Hill Cemetery *Park* in 1998. The park has a friends organization, it schedules regular birdwatching walks Sunday mornings during
peak migration season, and its trees and flowers serve as an outdoor
classroom for the many visiting school classes. (Cambridge's venerable
Mt. Auburn, meanwhile, remains a beautiful space with landscaping
specially designed to attract birds and butterflies, but it is privately
owned and very restrictively managed.)

In Portland, Maine, 236-acre municipally-owned Evergreen Cemetery is not only run by the city's park division but also happens to
be much larger than the city's largest "regular" park. Besides gardens,
ponds, open lawns, 65,000 gravesites, and 45,000 monuments, Evergreen also contains a 111-acre stand of primordial trees—the largest
and reputedly healthiest urban forest in the state of Maine. The cemetery is used for hiking, walking, running, biking, picnicking, cross-
country skiing, and snowshoeing. The warbler migration in May brings
millions of exotic birds and thousands of passionate watchers. Back in
the nineteenth century, when Evergreen was considered a full-fledged
destination, residents and tourists boarded trolleys for all-day excur-
sions to enjoy its combination of horticulture, history, and sculpture.
And the cemetery is becoming more park-like all the time. Most recently, a group called Portland Trails brought Evergreen directly into

the citywide trail network by constructing a path through the woods and linking it with an abandoned rail corridor and a waterfront route.

Atlanta's historic Oakland Cemetery, owned by the city's parks department and run by a foundation, is one of the city's oldest public spaces and offers a fascinating glimpse of the possibilities of a well-rounded cemetery park. Forty-eight-acre Oakland contains 70,000 graves (well above the rule of thumb 1,000 per acre), ranging from some of the city's most prominent citizens in large and elaborate monuments to Civil War casualties under neat rows of identical stones to thousands of unnamed indigents in two potter's fields. Since it had been the city's only cemetery for many years it also has small sections for Jews and African Americans. By the 1970s Oakland Cemetery (along with its wrong-side-of-the-tracks neighborhood) was in sad shape with overturned monuments, unmaintained trees, cracked roads and pathways, unkempt grass, and virtually nonexistent horticulture. Naturally, it was feared and largely shunned, but a small group of idealists had a dream of bringing it back. Just in time for the nation's bicentennial in 1976 they convinced Mayor Maynard Jackson to choose the facility as Atlanta's signature project.

Jackson had a big vision, according to Oakland's director of restoration and landscapes, Kevin Kuharic. "The mayor wanted to transform Oakland from a municipal expense to a municipal benefit." To do that, the private Historic Oakland Cemetery Foundation was created, and a formal management partnership was arranged with Atlanta Department of Parks, Recreation, and Cultural Affairs. As with virtually all successful public-private partnerships, ultimate authority remained in the hands of the city, but the foundation was given wide latitude on programming, publicity, and fundraising. The facility has been on a steady upward trajectory ever since, and its surrounding neighborhood has been following a similar rising arc. (Directly across the street now is a popular new gathering place, the Six Feet Under Pub and Fish House.)

Besides the usual cemetery fare of roads, walkways, and gravestones, Oakland has benches, gardens, and a small central building for events and programs. Over time, as funding permits, selected gardens are upgraded and beautified. In 2001, a water line was installed and drinking fountains added. Despite suffering a catastrophic direct hit by a tornado in 2008, Oakland retains an impressive collection of specimen trees, some dating back to the 1880s. Visitors are allowed to bicycle and jog, and, as with any other Atlanta park, they can picnic and stroll with their dogs (on leash). The foundation offers or encourages tours, photography classes, charity runs, a Halloween festival with period costumes and educational talks, and an annual Sunday in the Park festival with music, food, and crafts. Historically the cemetery has had only two entrances, on the south and west sides, but with the completion of a spate of new residential buildings near the east wall in the late 2000s, there has been discussion of adding a third way in and out, making the facility even more park-like.

With Oakland both a cemetery and a park, finding the proper balance is key. "Southerners are so proud of their history, they just want everyone to know about it," explained Kuharic. "But we're also fortunate that the cemetery is largely filled up. We have only about 12–15 burials a year, so inviting people in for the park ambience is what we're mostly about. If we're not having visitors, what's the point?"

Since the property is technically owned only 40 percent by the city and 60 percent by thousands of individual heirs, many of whom are not known, there have been some small controversies. One family that hadn't visited their ancestral plot in years was surprised to find a tree growing there. Kuharic was asked to cut it down, which he did. "That was painful," he said, "but they were within their rights."

As for the Halloween Tour, the propriety was negotiated. "Under our slogan of 'Enlighten, Don't Frighten,'" Kuharic said, "we've settled on a historic first-person format—an actor who educates. We get permission to open up four or five of the mausoleums every year, and as each group comes by, guided by tiki torches and luminaries along the pathways, an appropriately costumed character comes out to perform a historical tale. We sell timed tickets. It's so popular we now run it for three nights, and last year it brought in $45,000."

Obviously, maintaining a fragile facility with historic gravestones, mausoleums, specimen trees, and acres of lawns and shrubs is challenging. Historic Oakland Foundation has a membership of 850, a staff of seven, and a budget of about $1 million a year. Its work is supplemented by maintenance by the city parks department.

Another urban graveyard that operates essentially as a destination park is Old City Cemetery in Lynchburg, Virginia. Owned by the city and operated in partnership with the Southern Memorial Association, the cemetery has been in continuous use since 1806 and is a national historic site. Besides graves, it contains an extensive arboretum with an outstanding collection of antique roses; it has a working compost center that doubles as a facility for public education on composting; and it has numerous historical buildings, including a railroad station, a collection of antique hearses, a "Pest House" hospital from the Civil War, and a visitor center with a historical museum. A chapel is available for church services, funerals, and also weddings. The cemetery is open to the public daily from sunrise to sunset, tours are conducted weekly, and numerous special programs are conducted throughout the year including a rose festival, a Juneteenth music festival, wreath-making, Civil War and Revolutionary War walking tours, a candlelight tour, and a program on "bawdy ladies of nineteenth-century Lynchburg." The cemetery does not have a formal playground, but the city has attached an old-fashioned rope swing to one of the oak trees. The cemetery gets about 25,000 visitors a year, the great majority coming for the ambience rather than for visiting a particular gravesite. Maintained by Lynchburg's public works department staff (including a full-time horticulturist) and also supported by volunteers, Old City Cemetery is a park in every sense except for its name.

The latest development in the funeral business is the movement known as "green burial," a variety of practices that lessen the environmental impact of death—from foreswearing embalming chemicals, concrete vaults, large monuments, and pesticides to using only naturalistic design and native species, to providing special garden areas for scattering ashes. All these actions lead toward a more park-like ambience and less toward the traditional graveyard. While green burials are presently a largely rural phenomenon, the concept is spreading to cities. Colorado Springs plans to convert a 3-acre hillside within Fairview Cemetery to green interments in the near future.

No one knows the number of cemeteries in the nation, much less the number that are municipally operated. A directory compiled in the 1990s listed 22,000 cemeteries, but those were only the ones with current mailing addresses. Whatever the true number, it is obvious that the acreage is huge. However, just as obviously, utilizing a cemetery as a park is the exception rather than the rule; the majority keep tight control on allowed activities. The cemeteries in Lynchburg and Atlanta can be less restrictive because they get few first-generation family visitors who might complain about noise or disruption. Congressional Cemetery in Washington, D.C., is located in a tough neighborhood and had sunk to such a low level of upkeep that its board felt ready to try something radically innovative. To be successful as an urban park, a cemetery seems to require a private, nonprofit partner agency or a conservancy to provide extra funding, volunteers, programming, and publicity. If these multiple issues of policy and support can be worked out, cemeteries can serve as excellent green refuges in park-scarce neighborhoods and cities.

CHAPTER 22

Boulevards and Parkways

When the parkway was first invented by Frederick Law Olmsted and Calvert Vaux in the 1860s, it was much more a "park" and less a "way" than it is today. Of course, that was before the automobile. Eastern Parkway and Ocean Parkway, both in Brooklyn, New York, were wide boulevards with a center carriageway, narrow access roadways on each margin, and two attractive, maple-, oak-, ash-, and shrub-filled median malls for promenading, sitting, seeing, and being seen. The malls had a cinder equestrian trail. In 1894, the walkway on Ocean Parkway was split to form a bicycle path — the nation's first. There is also memorable paving work and even chess tables.

The concept was enticing for reasons of both beauty and economics: Parkways were not only pleasing to users but also provided a maximum amount of park edge upon which developers could construct homes. Many cities, from Buffalo to Chicago to Kansas City to Denver, eagerly followed suit. Over time, though, most urban parkways and boulevards have been chipped away by transportation engineers and modified by new regulations and insurance requirements so that they do more for cars and less for people. Some, like the Grand Concourse in New York, have essentially lost all vestiges of their original human element. Lanes were widened and speed limits raised. Trees were severely pruned or removed and not replanted, muscular guardrails were installed, and intrusive directional and regulatory signs erected. Meanwhile, on some older boulevards benches have been removed; on new ones they were never even contemplated. By the time of the automobile era, almost every aspect of parkway design was for windshield pleasure, not actual use.

Beautiful boulevards can provide ornamental breathing spaces for drivers and road-facing residents, but this is only the minimum return on the investment. With creativity, medians can do much more, serving as outstanding sitting, strolling, running, and dog-walking corridors. They could also be more effectively and intensively used through the addition of playgrounds, wading pools, chess boards, community gardens, or even some small-scale sports fields, such as badminton, horseshoes, bocce, shuffleboard, and other sports that are unlikely to interfere with traffic.

According to researchers at the University of Minnesota, making parkways into something more than just pretty roads requires that they be treated as places. "Parkways become places," they write, "by creating outdoor rooms that are shared by a broad community, not just the automobile. . . . The integration of sidewalks, bike paths, adjacent civic institutions, and other important cultural amenities with the road support the image of place. The orientation of buildings to the street also strongly influences the character of parkways."

Back in the nineteenth century, Eastern Parkway and Ocean Parkway served many different users, and even today they accommodate far more than just drivers. The 6-mile-long, 210-foot-wide Ocean Parkway contains about 110 acres of noncar space. Kansas City's Ward Parkway has spectacular fountains with benches, community-tended flower gardens, and Mirror Pool, which is used for ice-skating in midwinter. Boston's Commonwealth Avenue features a center walkway that has benches, public art, and monuments, along with majestic shade trees, bushes, and gardens. In contrast, the median on Pennsylvania Avenue in Southeast Washington, D.C., contains only small cherry trees and is designed solely as visual relief for drivers—it has no walkway, seating, or any other pedestrian-oriented amenity.

In Minneapolis, the city's famed 49-mile network of parkways known as the Grand Rounds mostly travels alongside streams, lakes, and the Mississippi River, but some stretches are stand-alone parkways that the city has moved to improve with more noncar facilities. St. Anthony Parkway was recently upgraded with a 3.5-mile, off-street bike trail plus gardens and plantings, lighting, and rest areas with water fountains, benches, and trash receptacles. Two rules that enhance the parkway's ambience are a ban on trucks and a 25 mile-per-hour speed limit.

Beyond squeezing more value out of existing parkways and boulevards, it may be possible to create new ones. Most cities have one or more streets that are extraordinarily and unnecessarily wide and that could be reconstructed as parkways with planted medians. This might be particularly effective in an old industrial area that formerly handled trucks or railcars but is now transforming into a residential or office district. Even urban highways are fair game for reconsideration. In many cities, the widest "streets" are the interstates that were bulldozed through preexisting neighborhoods and are now being reevaluated (see table 22.1). Unlike expressways, which serve as noisy, blighting barriers in cities, parkways are known to add substantial value to nearby residences, often resulting in enough additional tax revenue to cover the cost of their creation and maintenance. A study of two parkways in San Francisco that have been created where earthquake-damaged interstates were removed revealed that property values increased for a distance of a mile after the expressways were supplanted.

Many cities have made enhancements to existing focal streets by adding planted medians here and there. Some have large enough swaths of undeveloped or redevelopable land that they can design brand-new people-oriented parkways and boulevards as Denver is doing in its Stapleton neighborhood and Kansas City is doing in its outlying sections. But San Francisco is the only city that in recent times has rejuvenated existing streets as full-fledged new multiway boulevards—a new roadway with travel lanes, access lanes, and two park-like medians in between. Octavia Street had until 1999 been smothered by a never-completed stub of the elevated Central Freeway. When residents rose up and demanded the removal of the stub, a civic discussion arose over what to replace it with. Complex negotiations ensued between urban advocates and traffic engineers. The eventual outcome was abetted by the fact that two of the world's most knowledgeable experts on boulevard design happened to live in the San Francisco Bay area and were brought into the analysis. Allan B. Jacobs and Elizabeth MacDonald, coauthors of *The Boulevard Book*, helped design a road that had some of the attributes of the great European urban boulevards—lanes for faster-moving through traffic but also a park-like combination of thickly planted trees, a walking mall with brick pavers, and slow-speed lanes that allow for bicycling as well as cars. New shops and housing now dot the periphery, and a new 1-acre park acts as a conclusion. Octavia Street is modest but it does show that cities can retrofit sterile

Table 22.1   "Boulevardozing" Highways
Expressways Proposed for Conversion to Parkways

City	Highway
Baltimore	Jones Falls Expressway (part)
Bronx, N.Y.	Sheridan Expressway
Buffalo	Skyway
Louisville	Interstate 64 (part)
New Haven, Conn.	Route 34
New Orleans	Claiborne Expressway (part)
Oklahoma City	Interstate 40 (part)
Seattle	Alaskan Way Viaduct
Syracuse, N.Y.	Interstate 81 (part)
Trenton, N.J.	Route 29 (part)
Washington, D.C.	Southeast Freeway

Source: Congress on New Urbanism; The Trust for Public Land

streets into lively and human-oriented parkways. More grandiose is the Embarcadero, also in San Francisco, an extremely wide roadway with multiple lanes, multiple streetcar tracks, palm trees, sculpture, a farmers' market, fountains, and activity day and night. The elimination of the massive, double-decked Embarcadero Freeway got rid of a blighting architectural element, revealed the iconic Ferry Building in its splendor, and provided the city's eastern waterfront with perhaps the most extreme makeover of any spot in the United States, engendering hundreds of millions of dollars of redevelopment over a 2-mile stretch.

Minneapolis is now in the forefront of the parkway retrofit movement. While the city and the park board are justifiably proud of the Grand Rounds, that famous route is in fact also a bit of an embarrassment due to a 3-mile gap through the northeast quadrant of the city. The gap, and the decline of the area, has lasted for more than a century while real estate values (and social capital) in other sections of the city have flourished. After drawing up plans yet failing to fill the missing link in 1910, 1918, 1930, and 1939, the effort went dormant until 2007 when the Minneapolis Park and Recreation Board listed it among the top priorities in its comprehensive plan. A route has been selected that mostly involves using and redesigning existing roadways. There are formidable land acquisition challenges and a projected price tag in excess of $100 million, but the Park Board, under the slogan "Keeping the Promise," seems determined to achieve success. If and when it does, it will serve as an influential example that great parkways and boulevards are not only mementos from the past but can link recreation with transportation in the twenty-first century, too.

CHAPTER 23

Decking Highways

Urban radicals want automobiles banned. Urban moderates can perhaps live with cars as long as they're neither seen nor heard.

In European central cities the radicals have the upper hand. U.S. cities are increasingly settling for a compromise—an expensive compromise—by putting freeway segments underground and covering them with parkland (see table 23.1). Whether called a lid, deck, bridge, or tunnel, there are already at least twenty-four of these parks in the country and a dozen more somewhere in the planning pipeline. Surprisingly, because of both undulating topographies and the fact that many cities are already operating on multiple above- and below-ground levels, there are numerous opportunities to construct more freeway deck parks. As the impact of automobiles becomes ever less welcome in cities, these lids have moved from the novel to the accepted to, increasingly, the expected. The sometimes considerable cost has gone from being dismissed as "porkbarrel" to being redefined more positively as *amenity investment with high economic payback*.

In a study carried out by the Center for City Park Excellence in 2007, it was found that the average size of the nation's freeway parks is about 8 acres and each covers about 1,600 linear feet of highway. Most famous is Seattle's aptly named Freeway Park, designed by the Lawrence Halprin firm and opened with great fanfare in 1976, but the concept actually goes back to 1939 when Robert Moses constructed the Franklin D. Roosevelt Expressway along Manhattan's East River, tunneled it under the mayor's home at Gracie Mansion, and constructed 15-acre Carl Shurz Park on top. In 1950 Moses did it again, in Brooklyn, when citizens rose up against a planned expressway through the center of Brooklyn Heights. As a compromise he added the one-third-mile-long Brooklyn Promenade with its supreme view of lower Manhattan, remarking self-satisfiedly at the ribbon-cutting, "I don't

Table 23.1   Out of Sight, Out of Mind
Selected City Parks Constructed Over Highways

Park	City	Tunnel Length (linear feet)	Park Size (acres)	Highway
Riverwalk Plaza	Hartford, Conn.	158	1.5	I-91/I-84
Lytle Park	Cincinnati	528	2.3	I-71
Memorial Park	La Canada, Calif.	634	2.8	I-210
Waterside Park	Atlantic City, N.J.	2,112	3.0	Brigantine Blvd
Gateway Park	Arlington, Va.	792	3.7	I-66
Mid-City Bridge Park Deck	San Diego	370	4.0	I-15
Capitol Reflecting Pool	Washington, D.C.	2,376	5.0	I-395
Freeway Park	Seattle	528	5.2	I-5
I-95 Park & Memorial Parks (2 parks)	Philadelphia	1,056	5.5	I-95
South Riverwalk Park	Trenton, N.J.	898	6.5	U.S. 29
Hance Park	Phoenix	2,640	10.0	I-10
Carl Schurz Park	New York	1,584	14.9	FDR Drive
Sam Smith Park	Seattle	3,379	15.0	I-90
Rose Garden, Lake Place, Cooke Plaza (3 parks)	Duluth, Minn.	3,115	23.0	I-35
Rose Kennedy Greenway	Boston	5,280	30.0	I-93

know of anything quite like this in any city in the world." The latest have been New Jersey's innovative highway redesigns in Trenton and Atlantic City and the Rose Kennedy Greenway park blocks over Boston's massive "Big Dig."

The Interstate Highway System, when it was originally conceived in the early 1950s, was designed to link but not penetrate cities. By the 1960s, however, the distinction had been forgotten. Highways became the preeminent tool of urban renewal and redesign, and vast swaths of urban real estate were paved over. Waterfronts were blockaded in Portland, Oregon, Cincinnati, Hartford, Cleveland, Philadelphia, and San Francisco. Nooses of concrete were wound tightly around the downtowns of Dallas and Charlotte. Trenches of noise and smog cut through Boston, Detroit, Seattle, and Atlanta. Stupendous elevated structures threw shadows over Miami and New Orleans. And wide strips of land were taken from large, iconic parks in Los Angeles (Griffith Park), St.

Louis (Forest Park), Baltimore (Druid Hill Park), and San Diego (Balboa Park).

A few downtown parks actually survived the devastation thanks to the intervention of historic preservationists, including Lytle Park in Cincinnati and the National Mall in Washington, D.C. In both cases, citizen outcry forced the highway builders to tunnel underneath (although technically Lytle Park was leveled and then reconstructed three years later).

But it wasn't until the construction of Freeway Park that the "deck-the-freeway" concept began getting some serious attention. Because of the constrained, hourglass geography of Seattle, Interstate 5 was a particularly damaging road, and the environmentally oriented populace was dismayed by the impact. "There was a large moat of traffic between downtown and historically residential First Hill neighborhood," says Freeway Park Neighborhood Association President David Brewster. But the city was lucky—not only was I-5 sunk into a deckable trough as it passed downtown, but a former Seattle mayor, James "Dorm" Braman, had just been appointed assistant secretary of transportation for urban systems and the environment by President Richard Nixon. Braman was amenable to the deck, which was promoted by civic leader Jim Ellis and paid for under the city's "Forward Thrust" bond initiative. Freeway Park opened in time for the bicentennial and garnered coast-to-coast attention. "It was a model for other cities to heal the scar that cuts right through a neighborhood," says Brewster.

Freeway Park was beautiful and memorable, but it failed on one major count: acoustics. At 5 acres it couldn't completely muffle the sound of traffic, and the park experience is accompanied by a constant white noise—not obtrusive, but not minimal, either. Phoenix's 10-acre Hance Park seems to have solved the noise challenge (as has Seattle's new, much larger Sam Smith Park). Labeled by the Phoenix New Times "a rare Phoenix instance of nature over traffic—in this case, literally," Hance Park is decked over the Papago Freeway, uniting uptown and downtown and providing a park adjacent to the city's central library. The freeway (Interstate 10) was originally planned as an elevated bridge through downtown but opposition by citizens and the *Arizona Republic* killed that idea in a 1973 ballot measure. Not until ten years later did the city finally accept a below-grade solution with the park as a key sweetener. Hance Park opened in 1992 and today is the site of a Japanese garden. As a sign of success, it is gradually becoming surrounded by a growing number of upscale condominium towers.

Freeway parks have also bridged the divide between cities and their waterfronts. In Duluth, Minnesota, a plan to build Interstate 35 along the Lake Superior shoreline generated intense opposition from environmentalists and historic preservationists. By shortening the planned freeway's length (and gaining the backing of powerful Duluth thencongressman John Blatnik) the city used the savings to pay for park covers. Ultimately, three different deck parks were built, including one that saved a historic rose garden.

Construction costs for deck parks can be wincingly high, but there is also an upside—the land itself is generally free, made available through air rights by the state transportation agency. In center-city locations this can amount to a multimillion-dollar gift. Land near the Santa Ana Freeway by Los Angeles City Hall, for instance, goes for between $2 million and $3 million per acre. In near-downtown San Diego by Balboa Park an acre is worth up to $13 million. Regardless of cost, the actual force driving—and making feasible—most deck parks is the opportunity for neighboring private development and redevelopment. In Trenton, the New Jersey Department of Transportation spent $150 million on the new 6.5-acre Riverwalk deck over U.S. 29, linking the city to the Delaware River. In response, notes Trenton Planning Director Andrew Carten, "The project resulted in a significant spike in interest and the sale prices of property. After all, would you rather look over 600 trucks barreling past every day, or a scenic park and river?" One lot, worth $120,000 preconstruction, was developed with six housing units that sold for $200,000 each. The presence of the park also helped recruit a new 82-unit market rate residential building.

The cost of the Boston Central Artery—the gargantuan project to bury the elevated Fitzgerald Expressway that yielded as a surface byproduct the Rose Kennedy Greenway—has caused some people to doubt the feasibility of such parks in the future. But the Central Artery was primarily a transportation project that combined massive demolition along with even more massive construction. It also included major bridges and underwater tunnels. Of the $14-billion price tag, only an estimated $40 million was attributable to the mile-long stretch of four parks that opened to the public in October 2008. Certainly not inexpensive, but very much in line with many other new, showcase destination parks that are helping to redefine the nation's premier urban centers.

Projects where freeways are already below grade are more feasible, and four particularly high-prospect opportunities are currently being explored in St. Louis, Cincinnati, Dallas, and San Diego. In St. Louis, Mayor Francis Slay is promoting the "three-block solution," a plan to cover a portion of I-70 between center city and the world-famous Gateway Arch. "We're trying to get the annual 3 million visitors to the Arch into downtown St. Louis," says Peter Sortino, president of the Danforth Foundation, which is handling the planning. "We're also trying to help those already downtown more easily reach the Arch and the Mississippi riverfront." An early estimate put the cost at a minimum of $40 million. Cincinnati faces the identical situation. An interstate highway, Fort Washington Way, is a barrier between downtown and the parkland along the Ohio River. Cincinnati had an opportunity to construct a five-block-long park deck during a road reconstruction (and narrowing) in 2007, but shied away because of cost. As a compromise, the new Fort Washington Way was equipped with $10 million worth of steel pilings capable of supporting a future park.

Dallas, on the other hand, is plunging ahead with planning and funding a park over a stretch of the Woodall-Rodgers Freeway. The freeway separates the city's downtown and arts district from the Uptown neighborhood, and a three-block park cover is seen as both improving the urban form and opening up new opportunities for development. A trolley line would run through the park, and condominium towers are expected to flank it on both sides. A developer of a nearby tower is enthusiastic, telling the *Dallas Tribune* that the park "will be a fabulous amenity to [my] building." The park's price tag is estimated at more than $60 million, but Dallas's confident and ardent boosters are busily raising matching funds from private sources.

In San Diego, downtown interests are in the early stages of evaluating decking a few blocks of I-5 so as to forge a link with Balboa Park. The city has been in the midst of an unprecedented center-city residential construction boom, and the highway presents a major barrier for the thousands of apartment dwellers who have little access to green space. Meanwhile, activists in Los Angeles are determined not to lose their "Freeway-Capital-of-the-U.S." moniker and are evaluating eight different sites. "We want to now become the 'Freeway Deck Park Capital of the World,'" said Don Scott, chair of the Hollywood Central Park Coalition.

Despite the cost of a park deck, there are numerous sources of local, state, and federal funds that can be cobbled together, particularly if an analysis shows that associated development will generate significantly more tax revenue. Often the deck superstructure is paid for by the federal government while actual park development is financed by the city: Phoenix spent $5 million landscaping Hance Park. The Trenton deck came about through reconstruction of a state highway and was paid for by the state of New Jersey. In Cincinnati, 20 percent of the narrowing of Fort Washington Way was financed through private dollars, including $250,000 from the Cincinnati Bengals football team.

CHAPTER 24

Closing Streets and Roads

In every city there are hundreds of acres of streets and roadways potentially available as park and recreational facilities. While parks make up about 20 percent of New York City's total area, streets make up about 30 percent. In Chicago, 26 percent of the land is devoted to streets compared with only 8 percent for parks. Converting some street capacity for recreational activity—either full-time or part-time—is an underrealized opportunity.

Wresting space away from automobiles is never easy, but if any opportunities constitute "low-hanging fruit" they are the hundreds of miles of roads within city parks. Naturally, all large parks need some streets for access to facilities as well as to allow motorists to get from one side to the other, but most city parks have a surfeit of auto corridors. The National Mall in Washington, D.C., formerly had four parallel drives running for about a mile between the U.S. Capitol and the Washington Monument. Not only was the green Mall thoroughly intersected every few dozen yards by asphalt, but the drives themselves were permanently clogged with tourists (and government workers) looking for parking spaces. In 1976, just in time for the national bicentennial celebration, Assistant Interior Secretary Nathaniel Reed decided to abolish the two central roads and replace them with pebble-covered walkways reminiscent of those in Paris parks. The aggregate amount of space—about 4 acres—was relatively small, but the impact on park usability, ambience, safety, and air quality was monumental. Similarly, in Atlanta, following a raft of crime and nuisance issues that were negatively affecting Piedmont Park, Parks Commissioner Ted Mastroianni and Mayor Maynard Jackson announced test weekend road closures. Despite protests, the results led to dramatic increases in other uses of the park, such as running, walking, and cycling, and, in 1983 the closures were made total and permanent. (Piedmont Park is today the most car-free major city park in the United States.)

Other examples abound (see table 24.1). San Francisco's longtime Sunday closure of 2 miles of John F. Kennedy Drive in Golden Gate Park was extended in 2007 to Saturdays as well. The program, which makes available one of the only hard, flat, safe areas for children in the entire hilly city, according to the San Francisco Bike Coalition, effectively added about 12 acres of parkland without any acquisition or construction costs. Park usage during car-free hours is about double that of when cars are around. Even cities that are thoroughly oriented to cars are finding an enthusiastic constituent response to park road closures. Kansas City, Missouri, bans automobiles on beautiful Cliff Drive within Kessler Park from Friday noon until Monday morning during the summer. San Antonio permanently closed Brackenridge Park's Wilderness Road and Parfun Way in 2004. And Los Angeles has permanently closed 10 miles of Via del Valle and Mt. Hollywood Drive in Griffith Park to protect wildlife, reduce the risk of fire, and provide a safe, quiet venue for walkers, runners, and cyclists.

It's not just large parks. Many small parks that were disfigured by roads can be regreened, too. New York City's Washington Square, famous as a Greenwich Village movie set and also for street theater, rallies, and as a de facto quad for New York University, had been bisected by Fifth Avenue until 1964. Ironically, a proposal to expand that avenue into a freeway led to the uproar that made the park entirely car-free—and a much more successful space. In Washington, D.C., Thomas Circle had gradually been sliced down in size almost to the diameter of the statue of General George Henry Thomas and his horse, with traffic consuming the entire area. In 2007 the National Park Service and the District of Columbia reinstituted the original circle and rebuilt pedestrian walkways to allow people to use it. Earlier, a similar project reunified 2.5-acre Logan Circle and helped ignite a renewal of its neighborhood.

In 2007 Houston got itself a park addition by trading away a street. It happened in Hidalgo Park, a venerable 12-acre greenspace in the city's hard-bitten East End, near the Turning Basin on Buffalo Bayou where Houston started. When a small sliver between the park and the bayou came up for sale, the city secured federal funds to buy it through

Table 24.1 Do Not Enter

Park Roads that Have Been Closed to Automobiles, Selected Parks

Park	City	Road Name	Mileage	Closure Time	Year First Closed
Central Park	New York	Central Park Dr.	6	P	1966
Prospect Park	Brooklyn, N.Y.	Prospect Park Dr.	3.5	P	1966
Golden Gate Park	San Francisco	John F. Kennedy Dr.	2	P	1967
Gwynns Falls Trail	Baltimore	Ellicott Drive/Wetheredsville Rd.	6	F	1972
The National Mall	Washington, D.C.	Washington Dr. & Adams Dr.	2	F	1976
Audubon Park	New Orleans	Audubon Jogging Path	3.1	F	1980
Rock Creek Park	Washington, D.C.	Beach Dr.	4	P	1981
Fairmount Park	Philadelphia	Martin Luther King Dr.	4	P	1982
Piedmont Park	Atlanta	Piedmont Park Drive	2.9	F	1983
Washington Park	Denver	Marion Pkwy/Humboldt Dr.	2	F	1985
Overton Park	Memphis	Interior Rd.	2	F	1987
Griffith Park	Los Angeles	Mt. Hollywood Dr. & Vista del Valle	10	F	1991
Memorial Park	Houston	Picnic Loop	1.2	P	1994
Garden of the Gods	Colorado Springs	Gateway Road	0.25	F	1996
Brackenridge Park	San Antonio	Wilderness Rd. & Parfun Way	1	F	2004
Fair Park	Dallas	First Ave.	0.25	F	2004
Pope Park	Hartford, Conn.	Pope Park Dr.	0.2	F	2005
Franklin Mountains State Pk	El Paso	Scenic Drive	3	P	2008
Kessler Park	Kansas City, Mo.	Cliff Drive	2.6	P	2008
Hampton Park	Charleston, S.C.	Mary Murray Drive	1.5	P	n.a.

F—full-time; P—part-time; n.a.—not available

Source: Center for City Park Excellence, Trust for Public Land, 2008

an obscure federal program called Coastal and Estuarine Land Conservation. The sliver had two drawbacks: It was separated from Hildago Park by a street, plus there is a federal requirement that coastal funds be matched one-to-one by nonfederal dollars. Park Director Joe Turner took a tour of the site and had a "Eureka!" moment—why not close the street, have it transferred from the Public Works Department to Parks and Recreation, and use its land value as the local match for the federal grant? The politics and geography happened to be perfect: There were no houses on the street, it had no through access, and the one industrial user at the far end had another plant entrance it could use. And since no one before Joe Turner had ever offered to use the value of a street as a local match, the federal bureaucrats were surprised enough to say yes. (They've since rethought it and forbidden the maneuver, but the Houston handshake was grandfathered in.) Today Hidalgo Park is a much-improved 14 acres with unbroken access to the channel and views of the enormous ships coming up to the Turning Basin.

Closing and beautifying streets that are not in parks is more difficult. Many cities, including Boston, Santa Monica, and New Orleans, have turned one of their key downtown streets into a car-free zone, although in nearly all cases the motivation is less for casual, free recreation and clean air than for upscale shopping and dining. Portland, Oregon, however, did pull off a famous and extraordinarily successful "road-to-park" conversion. It involved the 1974 elimination of four-lane Harbor Drive, an expressway along the Willamette River that had been rendered redundant by a new interstate highway. Most cities would have given in to the strenuous remonstrances of their traffic engineers and kept highways along both sides of their river, but under the leadership of Mayor (later Governor) Tom McCall the old roadway was dug up and replaced by 37-acre Waterfront Park. The park opened in 1978, exactly three-quarters of a century after the concept was first proposed by planner and landscape architect Frederick Law Olmsted, Jr., in his plan for Portland. Built for about $8.5 million, the park in its very first year was credited with stimulating an estimated $385 million in retail, office, hotel, and residential development in the vicinity. Later named after the visionary governor, Tom McCall Waterfront Park has since become Portland's focal point for all kinds of activities and festivals.

Some cities, including Baltimore, El Paso, Chicago, New York, and Miami, have recently begun experimenting with the idea of once-a-

summer or once-a-month road closures on regular city streets, following the example of the "ciclovias" that have become immensely popular
in Bogotá, Colombia; Quito, Ecuador; and several other Latin American cities. Called such things as "Summer Streets," "Scenic Sundays,"
"Walk and Roll," and "Bike Days Miami," the events often take place
on cities' most park-like streets (Park Avenue in New York, Scenic Drive
in El Paso) and bring forth tens of thousands of people in an electrifying, community atmosphere in a domain normally dominated by cars.
(The events are often initially organized and promoted by bicyclists but
soon become so congested that they evolve into street festivals.)

Cities can permanently convert streets into park-like "Woonerfs,"
a Dutch concept for neighborhood ways where pedestrians, bicyclists,
and children are given priority over cars. (The name translates to "Home
Zone," which is what it is called in Great Britain.) While the concept
has yet to fully establish itself in the United States, variants have sur-
faced. On downtown Asheville, North Carolina's, Wall Street, the city
installed brick pavers, bollards, benches, and lights so intertwined that
they become an obstacle course that greatly reduces automobile speeds.
Seattle is doing similar traffic calming in certain neighborhoods and is
also adding numerous pervious areas and water-capturing features to
add ecological benefits to these "street-parks."

CHAPTER 25

Removing Parking

Do you park in your park? Does it seem to be a parking lot more than a park, a lot? Can one even write on this topic without getting tangled by the clashing meanings of the same word?

Urban park advocates struggle mightily to create new green space through a precious parcel here and an irreplaceable acre there. But a large swath of existing parkland is given over to the prosaic task of automobile storage, complete with its side impacts—impermeable surface, water runoff and erosion, oil drippings, heat island effect, displacement of trees and meadows, and loss of playing area. A 2007 study by the Center for City Park Excellence (CCPE) of seventy major city parks in the United States revealed that, collectively, they devote a total of 529 acres to the very technology that many people seek to escape when they head into their local patch of nature. That's an area larger than Schenley Park in Pittsburgh, City Park in Denver, Lake Harriet Park in Minneapolis, or Franklin Park in Boston. In Chicago, where the city spent $475 million to create 24-acre Millennium Park, almost twice that much land—46 acres—is given over to auto storage within nearby Lincoln Park.

On average, CCPE found that signature urban parks provide slightly more than one auto space for every acre of parkland. The range is from almost zero spaces in Brooklyn's Prospect Park to more than 6,000 in Chicago's Lincoln Park, more than 7,000 in St. Louis's Forest Park, and 10,000 in Flushing Meadow/Corona Park in New York (see table 25.1).

Storing an unused car requires approximately 330 square feet (0.008 acre), according to Donald Shoup, professor of Urban Planning at University of California at Los Angeles and author of *The High Cost of Free Parking*. This factors in the actual surface area of the auto plus the extra

Table 25.1   Pavement in Paradise
Acres for Auto Storage in Selected Parks (Surface Spaces Only)

Park	City	Acres	No. of Spaces	Acres Occupied by Parking	Auto Spaces per Acre of Parkland
Woodward Park	Fresno, Calif.	300	2,500	18.9	8.3
Flushing Meadow/ Corona Park	New York	1,255	10,000	75.8	8.0
Forest Park	St. Louis	1,293	7,875	59.7	6.1
Overton Park	Memphis	342	1,800	13.6	5.3
Garfield Park	Indianapolis	123	630	4.8	5.1
Lincoln Park	Chicago	1,212	6,051	45.8	5.0
Freedom Park	Charlotte	105	482	3.7	4.6
Hermann Park	Houston	445	2,000	15.2	4.5
National Mall	Washington, D.C.	146	570	4.3	3.9
Golden Gate Park	San Francisco	1,018	3,760	28.5	3.7
Trinity Park	Fort Worth	193	709	5.4	3.7
Balboa Park	San Diego	1,091	3,778	28.6	3.5
Schenley Park	Pittsburgh	426	1,240	9.4	2.9
Centennial Park	Nashville	126	275	2.1	2.2
Mount Trashmore	Virginia Beach, Va.	165	350	2.7	2.1
Brackenridge Park	San Antonio	347	732	5.5	2.1
Zilker Park	Austin	382	633	4.8	1.7
Franklin Park	Boston	453	700	5.3	1.5
Washington Park	Portland, Ore.	222	325	2.5	1.5
Griffith Park	Los Angeles	4,171	5,695	43.1	1.4
Lake Park	Milwaukee	137	156	1.2	1.1
Piedmont Park	Atlanta	171	150	1.1	0.9
Cherokee Park	Louisville	314	242	1.8	0.8
Central Park	New York	840	130	1.0	0.2
Prospect Park	Brooklyn, N.Y.	526	40	0.3	0.1

Source: Center for City Park Excellence, The Trust for Public Land

space for aisles required to maneuver in and out of an enclosure. For a 500-car lot, that comes to four acres. Of course, Americans assume they have the right to drive, one person per car, from home to a space directly next to a tennis court, rose garden, or picnic table—at least until it's pointed out that 100 percent auto access means 0 percent park. Despite the popular assumption, auto storage doesn't correlate directly with visitation. The nation's most heavily used park, Central Park in New York, has only 130 parking spaces yet gets 25 million visits per year. Prospect Park in Brooklyn, New York, receives 6 million visits while providing only forty spaces for skaters at Wollman Rink— and that lot is open only periodically. On the other hand, in Houston, about 15 of Hermann Park's 445 acres are devoted to 2,000 spaces for automobile storage (about 4.5 spaces per acre). Interestingly, though it gets about 2.3 million visits per year, Hermann is less heavily used than Riverside Park in New York, which has almost no auto storage.

"On about fifty days per year there is no possible way to meet the demand, and on another fifty we're right at the limit for capacity," says Rick Dewees, administrator of Hermann Park. Nevertheless, he points out, "It's hard to add spaces when the lots are empty three-fourths of the time." Dewees has been forced to become a bit thick-skinned about the issue: "You're always going to have people complaining there isn't enough parking during peak times," he says.

Parks surrounded by low-density housing with little or no mass transportation and filled with high-intensity sports facilities are under relentless pressure to provide large amounts of space for cars. But not every park is held hostage by the automobile. Parks with many people living or working in close proximity and a range of good transit options nearby are able to succeed with little or no car storage. Nevertheless, battles over the issue rage from coast to coast. Two of the more instructive took place in Piedmont Park, Atlanta, and Golden Gate Park, San Francisco.

Of the nation's big-city signature parks, Piedmont Park is relatively small, making an internal auto repository particularly undesirable. There is one open-air lot, but no curbside spaces, since the city closed all Piedmont's internal roadways to cars in 1983. The park is fairly well-served by transit, but overflow autos end up in the surrounding neighborhood, which is wealthy, organized, outspoken, and unhappy about the traffic. Also in Piedmont Park is the Atlanta Botanical Garden, which has the same automobile problem but a bit more financial wherewithal to do something about it. The Garden's original proposal to construct a multilevel garage in an underused portion of the park generated shock and opposition, but gradually a broad compromise was crafted, and in 2008 an 800-car garage was built relatively inconspicuously in a steep, wooded hillside. In return, the Piedmont Park Conservancy removed the existing open-air lot and also added more park entrances for walkers and cyclists. Serving both Botanical Garden visitors and Piedmont Park users (with the Garden covering the costs of construction and operation), the garage charges $1.75 per hour, which came as a jolt to auto-oriented Atlantans, but has not materially reduced attendance. Some users mitigated the price by carpooling; others shifted modes to foot, bicycle, subway, or bus; most simply paid the car storage cost, recognizing that the park experience is worth it. (It doesn't hurt that Piedmont Park has been in the midst of a multiyear, multimillion-dollar upgrade that is raising it to the status of top-tier urban park.)

In San Francisco, Golden Gate Park (not to be confused with Golden Gate National Recreation Area, which is mostly outside the city) is a 1,017-acre pleasure ground of forests, ponds, meadows, gardens—and 28.5 acres of storage space for 3,760 cars. One reason for all the cars is the de Young Museum of Art, located in the park. When the venerable museum needed major renovation in the 1990s, the board explored moving the collection to a more transit-accessible location downtown. But some San Franciscans couldn't imagine the park without the museum and raised an outcry. Meanwhile, bicyclists and conservationists were adamant that if the de Young stayed there would have to be a reduction of automobile asphalt. After much wrangling, a compromise was reached. The de Young would remain, a public-private consortium would construct an 800-space underground garage, and the city would remove an equivalent number of spaces from the park's surface.

It took seven years and two lawsuits, but in 2005 the $55-million garage opened, funded by private contributions and built by the public Golden Gate Park Concourse Authority. Abiding by the agreement, 837 surface auto spaces (worth about 6.5 acres) were then eliminated. (Using the garage in 2009 cost $2.50 per hour, $3 on weekends.)

There are three ways to reduce the problem of car storage in city parks. One involves an economic stick, two involve structural carrots. Naturally, none of them is painless.

By far the simplest and most effective response is to charge a parking fee. Storing a car in a park is a service with value. Doing so also places many human and environmental costs on the park system. With an equation like that, a payment should work. Unfortunately, two deep-seated cultures are in conflict on this issue—the underlying commitment to free-market capitalism versus the common expectation of free city services. And if something is free for you, then you assume it's free for your car, too, right?

Most of the high-population-density cities don't try to meet auto demand, relying on residents to walk, use transit or bikes, or pay to use private garages nearby. Most of the low-density cities don't challenge the car culture and don't necessarily get enough usership in any one park for it to be an overwhelming problem. It is in the mid-density cities that the issue often comes to a head. Minneapolis has taken the lead in charging for cars, probably because it has an independent park and recreation board that can set its own fees and is less constrained by normal city council politics. After a failed ten-year experiment with an honor system in the busiest of its six regional parks, the Park Board installed meters, charging between 50 cents and $1.25 per hour, depending upon demand. (The high end of the scale is for parks near downtown and near the University of Minnesota.) Because the Park Board receives all the meter revenue, it can determine how the money ($795,000 in 2005) is used. According to Don Siggelkow, a general manager with the board, some of the funds go for park maintenance and some for youth athletics. But recognizing the issue's volatility, the Park Board bends over backward to make auto payments as light a task as possible, offering an annual Patron Pass for $27. Moreover, violators who are ticketed can opt to avoid the fine *ex post facto* by upgrading to one of the passes. Pittsburgh's Schenley Park, located near the University of Pittsburgh, also has some meters, although the revenue flows to the city's general fund rather than to the park itself.

The flip side of the coin, of course, is to provide park users with transit options. Eight of the ten most heavily used city parks have subway or light-rail access within one-quarter mile, and all of them have bus service that comes even closer. Outside of New York City (where almost all parks have subway service), among the parks best served by rail are Boston Common, Forest Park in St. Louis, Grant Park in Chicago, Centennial Olympic Park in Atlanta, and the National Mall in Washington, D.C. Naturally, instituting transit service, especially rail, to major parks is expensive. But it is not out of the question. In Houston, the city's first light-rail line, opened in January 2004, features two stops in Hermann Park. This outcome wasn't a given. Planners had known that they wanted to run the tracks between downtown and the Reliant Park stadium, but the intermediary route had several different possible alignments. "We lobbied hard to get service for the park," said the park department's Dewees, "and we consistently supported that alignment through the planning process. Now we see quite a few people using rail to get here."

Conversely, in Chicago, when the Chicago Transit Authority proposed eliminating service on its Green Line elevated train, a broad coalition of community leaders, including Eunita Rushing of the Garfield Park Conservatory Alliance, rose up in opposition, claiming in part that the shutdown would negatively affect people's ability to get to Garfield Park and would also add automobiles to the neighborhood. The line was saved.

At Washington Park in Portland, Oregon, home to the popular Rose and Japanese Gardens, cars and buses regularly exceed the auto storage capacity from May through September. The city, according to Park Manager Bob Stilson, is unwilling to add to the 86 spaces (though it is unwilling to charge for them, either). In response to the crunch, Tri-Met, the regional transit agency, has added a peak-season bus that shuttles between eight stops within the 130-acre park and the closest MAX light-rail stop. The service, which runs every 15 minutes and costs $1.70 (or is free with a transfer), is aggressively advertised by the park department, Tri-Met, and event promoters. The route gets about 500 riders per day on weekends and 420 on weekdays.

Which leads to the third way of reducing auto storage problems in parks: increasing population density nearby. For every person who lives within walking distance of a park, one fewer needs to drive and deal with a car when she gets there. Comparison in point: New York's Riverside Park and Fresno's Woodward Park. Both are approximately the same size (325 and 300 acres, respectively) but Riverside has only 120 parking spaces while Woodward has 2,500. The difference is in the surrounding neighborhoods (see table 25.2). Riverside has the Hudson River on one side and a solid row of twelve- and sixteen-story buildings on the other. And behind those buildings are many blocks alternating three-story brownstones with large apartment buildings. Woodward, in contrast, is bordered by single-family homes, most of which have lots large enough for pools, on cul-de-sac street layouts. The residential population density around Woodward is about 6.5 persons per acre, virtually guaranteeing heavy reliance on autos to get to the park. The density around Riverside Park is about 180 persons per acre, higher than any other park studied by the Center for City Park Excellence. According to Jim Dowell, president of the Riverside Park Fund, most users of the park walk from within about four blocks.

Obviously, adding residential (or commercial) density around parks is not a short-term project. Nor is it noncontroversial. People who live in single-family homes on large lots around large parks enjoy their

Table 25.2   Living on the Edge
Population Density Surrounding Selected City Parks

Park	City	Park Size (acres)	Persons within 500 Feet of Park	Population Density Around Park (persons per acre)
Riverside Park	New York	325	63,850	178
Central Park	New York	840	55,199	142
Lincoln Park	Chicago	971	51,270	93
Golden Gate Park	San Francisco	1,018	22,254	41
Franklin Park	Boston	472	7,377	34
Rock Creek Park	Washington, D.C.	1,969	23,595	22
Balboa Park	San Diego	1,060	8,258	19
Green Lake Park	Seattle	323	2,681	15
Fairmount Pk/ Wissahickon Valley	Philadelphia	4,237	29,856	13
Piedmont Park	Atlanta	170	1,928	12
Washington Park	Denver	155	1,763	10
Lake Harriett Park	Minneapolis	119	2,053	10
Garfield Park	Indianapolis	123	1,258	9
Griffith Park	Los Angeles	3,157	5,167	4
Forest Park	Portland, Ore.	4,317	1,379	1

Population data, 2005
Source: Center for City Park Excellence, The Trust for Public Land

quality of life (especially if they can prevent outsiders from parking in their neighborhood), and they understandably want to maintain it. However, a case can be made that increasing density—allowing the construction of multistory apartment buildings on and near the edges of parks—unlocks a great deal of value for the benefit of the whole city. The benefits include more property tax revenue, the likelihood of healthier citizens because of park views and use, and the ability to reduce the presence of stored automobiles in parks.

CHAPTER 26

Adding Hours Rather than Acres

Finally, if not enough land can be amassed in the first three dimensions, there is always a fourth one: time. Cities are finding that, through the use of technology, the time that parks are available to the citizenry can be extended. For sports and other recreational activities, buying time can literally be the equivalent of buying land.

The two principal time-extending approaches utilize sports field lights and artificial playing surfaces (synthetic turf). Both are growing in importance in crowded environments.

Lighting has the longer history, and most cities already have numerous lit facilities, including tennis and basketball courts and baseball, football, and soccer fields. Oakland has seventeen lit fields and a policy that all new fields will include lights. Atlanta has forty-four. Miami, which has an extreme park shortage plus a 365-days-per-year playing season (and which, during the summer, is much more pleasant at night), illuminates almost everything: twenty-six baseball diamonds; eleven soccer, six football, and five combination fields; and even one cricket pitch. On the other end of the climate spectrum, Minneapolis lights a golf course for nighttime cross-country skiing in the snows of winter.

Because of lights, usable playing time can be extended by about two hours in the height of summer and up to five hours in the depth of winter. (Most park agencies have an outdoor nighttime sports curfew of 10:00 or 10:30 p.m.) Even ruling out the very coldest months, the average city might pick up almost 1,000 hours of extra sports playing time for every lit field.

And, despite the energy crunch, night lighting is still economical in comparison to land acquisition—at least wherever land is expensive. Installing an illumination system on a field costs about $150,000 (or half that for tennis or basketball), to which must be added an hourly operating cost from about $5 to $20, depending on electricity rates in each city. Most cities tend to reserve the lit fields for permitted high school and league competitions, although they allow pick-up games at other times. Some allow free use, others don't. Miami charges $10 per hour, Atlanta has a sliding scale all the way up to $71 per hour, depending whether teams are nonprofit and whether they are composed of city or noncity residents. The lights have a variety of operating systems, from old-fashioned manual control by onsite custodians to the latest in cellphone-activated, passcode-protected remote electronic management.

Lights can be controversial with neighbors, depending on the location of the park and layout of the fields. However, new technology seems to be helping there, too, thanks to the invention of better methods to focus the beam and reduce ambient light and glare. Fortunately, on this score there are no trade-offs: the less light "spillage," the less the operating costs. A major sports illumination company, Musco Lighting, claims that it can cut both hourly costs and unwanted glare by 50 percent simply through the use of better designed luminaires, the bonnets that direct the light onto fields and away from others' eyes. (Reducing the cost means less electricity used and less pollution generated, although lights, of course, do have a somewhat negative environmental impact.) There are still issues of activity, noise, cars, and ambient nighttime light, but for every complainant, someone else approves of a park that is busy and activated in the evening and that does not serve as a dark gathering place for clandestine, antisocial uses.

Lighting can also extend the hours for other parkland uses beyond traditional competitive sports on fields. The Midtown Greenway in Minneapolis and the Lieberman Exercise Trail in Houston's Memorial Park are both lighted for bicycling and running, and both facilities are approaching round-the-clock use (the Midtown Greenway because it gets lots of purposeful transportation use, and the Lieberman Trail because parking at Memorial Park is so difficult that runners start showing up at 4:30 a.m. just to get a space).

Synthetic turf is a much newer development that can also dramatically increase a park field's usable hours. This is not "Astroturf," the first-generation artificial material that was created to deal with the problem that grass wouldn't grow in the domed baseball stadium built for the Houston Astros in 1965. Early products were more rug-like and drew complaints for injuries, ambient temperature, ball handling, and water runoff. Several technological generations later, current synthetics come much closer to mimicking real grass, cause far fewer athletic injuries than older versions, and seem to be strongly supported by coaches, players, and park department officials. By allowing a field to be played upon continuously without any rest, artifical turf extends playing hours on a morning-to-night basis as well as month to month.

"Our natural grass fields are so old and so heavily used that in many places they've turned to bare dirt," explained Mark Oliver, special assistant to the director of the Oakland Department of Parks and Recreation. "In dry weather that means dust, in wet weather it means mud." Artificial turf has no such limitation. "We can use them twelve months a year," Oliver said.

In Boston, with cold and snow sometimes keeping players out of parks in the depth of winter, the season for artificial turf is a bit shorter—generally March through December. But again it is significantly longer than with grass. "Up here, grass fields are unplayable in the spring," said Stanley Ivan, director of design and construction with the Boston Parks and Recreation Department. "March and even April are very iffy for us with the wet weather."

The hour-by-hour use is also extended.

"We are real happy with the FieldTurf as it is virtually maintenance-free," said City of Miami Park Manager Jose Leiva. "The high schools love it and we increased our number of games we can hold on the turf by almost four times compared to what we were able to accommodate with natural grass, which is incredible."

The downside is that synthetic turf is expensive—as much as $1.5 million per field, counting the price of preparation, materials, and installation. On the other hand, once the initial cost is covered, day-to-day maintenance is easier and cheaper. There is no mowing, no use of fertilizers or herbicides, and no irrigation (although the fields do need occasional hosing down and washing). Healthwise, the new technology seems to be a trade-off: more injuries due to foot-twisting, fewer due to falling into holes; more injuries from "turf burn," fewer from concussions. As for its environmental ramifications, the verdict is still out. The latest synthetics are designed to allow much rainwater to percolate through the matting to the ground underneath, although they are probably not quite as pervious as natural lawns. Not needing fertilizer and herbicides is a major bonus for clean water and human health;

on the other hand, the dust given off by embedded pulverized rubber granules, or by painted nylon fibers, may be harmful to users, and several state health departments have been monitoring the air around some of these fields.

Another technology that is helping to extend the hours of park use, both daytime and evening, is the video camera. Obviously, cameras in parks are not an ideal solution, but their presence does help people feel more secure in rougher neighborhoods, and anything that keeps parks more populated begins a virtuous cycle of use and safety. In MacArthur Park in Los Angeles, police credit the installation of cameras (plus a partial park renovation) with reducing drug dealing and crime and bringing more of the community into the famous and iconic park.

Almost every other aspect of city life is moving toward a "24/7" schedule, so it is not surprising that recreation and park use is, too (although we will probably never again see a time when thouasands of residents grab pillows and sheets to sleep out in city parks on hot summer nights, as they did in the 1930s and as was portrayed in the movie *Avalon*). The scarcity of land and facilities inexorably pushes park managers to maximize the efficiency with which scarce resources can be used, and adding hours to the day, and days to the year, is another way to please the crowds.

Conclusion

This is an exciting time for those who love urban parks, but it is also a perilous moment. With so much new attention—and new investment—being lavished on cities, park development and redevelopment must be done right. For many years the danger to parks was of collapse from disinvestment and abandonment; now the risk is from inundation and overuse. Yes, urbanism is on the rebound, but it can't be an exact replica of the old urbanism. That kind of development, after all, posed enough problems and frustrations for residents to lead to a powerful and disastrous post–World War II anticity movement.

The futures of our nation and of our planet are inextricably tied to the future of our urban areas, yet, in a can't-live-with-them-can't-live-without-them conundrum, people everywhere are conflicted about their cities. After all, it is amid the crowds and stresses of the city that the latest challenges always arise and that the resulting solutions are always tested. The challenge addressed in this book—the shortage of urban natural spaces and people places—is a critical impediment to strengthening cities and reducing exurban sprawl. The solutions are all in various stages of being tested—horticulturally, ecologically, sociologically, financially, and politically. Each has demonstrated success at least once, somewhere, sometime. A few, like rooftop parks and reservoir decks, are in their infancy; others, like community gardens and rails-to-trails conversions, have proven themselves a thousand times or more. At this juncture it is impossible to know which innovations will thrive in cities of tomorrow, which will be discarded, and what other ideas will emerge.

Yet it must be admitted that most cities are still far from having outstanding park systems. The reason, I believe, is twofold. First, as we have seen, maintaining a great park is just plain difficult—perhaps the most difficult task in a city (even though, ironically, the average citizen innocently thinks nothing could be easier). Second is the insularity of the park community itself. Too many advocates define themselves within the boundary of their parks and not by the context in which they sit. While many go to city council meetings and angrily demand budget increases by claiming that "all great cities have great parks," it is closer to the truth to say that "great parks have great cities." Cities are extraordinarily complicated, and getting anything done requires leaders and activists with unusual stamina, creativity, and communication skills. Advocates who end up talking among themselves will not be successful unless they recognize that many citizens have fears and concerns about parks and urban public space. Only by working cooperatively with the many other constituencies in the city will advocates ever get to the point where a mayor's traditional directive to a park superintendent—"Do more with less"—is replaced with the liberating permission to "Do more with more!"

There are powerful economic and social forces at work in our cities; park advocates can confidently assert themselves in this fray. Parks are the beautiful and animated spaces around which everyone else can build their structures, house their residents, welcome their workers, lure their tourists, and teach their children. Park lovers have struggled through decades of bad politics, missed connections, lost opportunities, and fading beauty. We are now finally in a place where new ideas and new parks can flourish.

Recommended Reading

Urban Park History, Philosophy, and Analysis

Beveridge, Charles, and Paul Rocheleau. *Frederick Law Olmsted: Designing the American Landscape*. New York: Universe, 1998.

Cranz, Galen. *The Politics of Park Design: A History of Urban Parks in America*. Cambridge: MIT Press, 1989.

Czerniak, Julia, and George Hargreaves. *Large Parks*. Princeton Architectural Press, 2007.

Garvin, Alexander. *A Parks Agenda for the Twenty-First Century*. Ashburn, Va.: National Recreation and Park Association, 1999.

———. Parks and playgrounds. In *The American City: What Works, What Doesn't*, Alexander Garvin, 31–59. New York: McGraw-Hill, 1996.

Garvin, Alexander, Gayle Berens, and Christopher B. Leinberger, et al. *Urban Parks and Open Space*. Washington, D.C.: Urban Land Institute, 1997.

Harnik, Peter. *Inside City Parks*. Washington, D.C.: Urban Land Institute, 2000.

Heckscher, August. *Open Spaces: The Life of American Cities*. New York: Harper & Row, 1976.

Jacobs, Jane. The uses of neighborhood parks. In *The Death and Life of Great American Cities*, Jane Jacobs, 116–146. New York: The Modern Library, 1961.

Tate, Alan. *Great City Parks*. Spon Press, 2001.

Park and Recreation Standards and Planning

Buechner, Robert D. *National Park Recreation and Open Space Standards*. Washington, D.C.: National Recreation and Park Association, 1971.

Butler, George D. *Municipal and County Parks in the U.S., 1940: A Report of a Study Conducted by the National Park Service with the Cooperation of the American Institute of Park Executives and the National Recreation Association*. National Recreation and Park Association, 1940.

Fogg, George E. *Park Planning Guidelines, 3rd Edition*. National Recreation and Park Association, Ashburn, Va., 1981.

French, Jere Stuart. *Urban Green: City Parks of the Western World*. Dubuque, Iowa: Kendall/ Hunt Publishing Company, 1973.

Harnik, Peter. *The Excellent City Park System: What Makes It Great and How to Get There*. San Francisco: The Trust for Public Land, 2006.

Lewis, Megan, ed. *From Recreation to Re-creation: New Directions in Parks and Open Space System Planning*. Chicago: American Planning Association, 2008.

Mertes, James D., and James R. Hall. *Park, Recreation, Open Space and Greenway Guidelines*. Ashburn, Va.: National Recreation and Park Association, 1995.

National Park Service for the Land Planning Committee of the National Resources Board. *Recreational Use of Land in the United States: Part XI of the Report on Land Planning*. Washington, D.C.: U.S. Government Printing Office, 1938.

Weir, Lebert Howard. *Parks: A Manual of Municipal and County Parks*. New York: A.S. Barnes, 1928.

Buying Parkland

Hopper, Kim, and Ernest Cook. *The Conservation Finance Handbook*. Washington, D.C.: Trust for Public Land, 2004.

McQueen, Mike, and Edward McMahon. *Land Conservation Financing*. Washington, D.C.: Island Press, 2003.

The Trust for Public Land. LandVote® Database 2009. www.landvote.org.

Rooftop Parks

Green Roofs for Healthy Cities North America. www.greenroofs.org.

Community Gardens

Lawson, Laura J. *City Bountiful: A Century of Community Gardening in America*. Berkeley: University of California Press, 2005.

Seattle Department of Neighborhoods. P-Patch Community Gardens. www.seattle.gov/ Neighborhoods/ppatch.

Voicu, Ioan, and Vicki Been. The effect of community gardens on neighboring property values. *Real Estate Economics* vol. 36, no. 2 (Summer 2008): 241–83.

Developer Exactions

Harnik, Peter, and Laura J. Yaffe. *Who's Going to Pay for This Park? The Role of Developer Exactions in the Creation of New City Parks*. White paper. Washington, D.C., Trust for Public Land, 2005. Available at www.tpl.org/content_documents/ccpe_who_is _going_to_pay.pdf.

Landfills to Parks

Harnik, Peter, Michael Taylor, and Ben Welle. From dumps to destinations: The conversion of landfills to parks. *Places* vol. 18, no. 1 (Spring 2006): 83–88.

Parkways and Boulevards

Jacobs, Allan B., Elizabeth MacDonald, and Yodan Rofé. *The Boulevard Book: History, Evolution, Design of Multiway Boulevards*. Cambridge: MIT Press, 2002.

Schoolyard Parks

Boston Schoolyard Initiative. www.schoolyards.org.
Houston School Park Program. www.sparkpark.org.

Denver Learning Landscapes Program. Learning Landscapes, University of Colorado Denver, P.O. Box 173364, Campus Box 126, Denver, CO 80202; 303-352-3636.

Rail Trails

Nevel, Bonnie, and Peter Harnik. *Railroads Recycled: How Local Initiative and Federal Support Launched the Rails-to-Trails Movememnt, 1965–1990.* Washington, D.C.: Rails-to-Trails Conservancy, 1990.

Ryan, Karen-Lee, ed. *Trails for the Twenty-First Century: Planning, Design, and Management Manual for Multi-Use Trails, Second Edition.* Washington, D.C.: Island Press, 2001.

Ryan, Karen-Lee, and Julie A. Winterich. *Secrets of Successful Rail-Trails.* Washington, D.C.: Rails-to-Trails Conservancy, 1993.

Cemetery Parks

Green Burial Council. www.greenburialcouncil.org.

Automobile Parking

Shoup, Donald. *The High Cost of Free Parking.* Chicago: Planners Press, 2005.

Density and Nearby Value

Campoli, Julie, and Alex S. MacLean. *Visualizing Density.* Cambridge, Mass.: Lincoln Institute of Land Policy, 2007.

Crompton, John L. 2004. *The Proximate Principle: The Impact of Parks, Open Space and Water Features on Property Values and the Property Tax Base.* Ashburn, Va.: National Recreation and Park Association.

Forsyth, Ann. *Measuring Density: Working Definitions for Residential Density and Building Intensity.* University of Minnesota, Design Center for the American Urban Landscape, Design Brief No. 8, July 2003.

Appendix 1

Population Density, Largest Cities

City	Area (acres)	Population (2007)	Population Density (persons per acre)
High-Density Cities			
New York	195,072	8,310,212	42.6
San Francisco	29,884	764,976	25.6
Jersey City	9,600	242,389	25.2
Santa Ana, Calif.	17,280	339,555	19.7
Boston	30,992	608,352	19.6
Chicago	145,362	2,836,658	19.5
Miami	22,830	424,662	18.6
Newark, N.J.	15,360	280,135	18.2
Philadelphia	86,456	1,449,634	16.8
Washington, D.C.	39,297	588,292	15.0
Long Beach	32,281	466,520	14.5
Los Angeles	300,201	3,834,340	12.8
Baltimore	51,714	640,150	12.4
Intermediate High-Density Cities			
Oakland	35,875	401,489	11.2
Seattle	53,677	594,210	11.1
Minneapolis	35,130	377,392	10.7
Anaheim	31,360	333,249	10.6
Buffalo	26,240	272,632	10.4
Detroit	88,810	916,952	10.3
St. Louis	39,630	355,663	9.0
Cleveland	49,650	438,042	8.8
Pittsburgh	35,573	311,218	8.7
San Jose	111,910	939,899	8.4
St. Paul	33,920	277,251	8.2
Stockton	35,200	287,245	8.2
Intermediate Low-Density Cities			
Las Vegas	72,514	558,880	7.7
Sacramento	62,180	460,242	7.4
Glendale, Ariz.	35,840	253,152	7.1
Fresno	66,791	470,508	7.0
Chandler, Ariz.	36,480	246,399	6.8

continued

Appendix 1, continued

City	Area (acres)	Population (2007)	Population Density (persons per acre)
Cincinnati	49,898	332,458	6.7
St. Petersburg	38,400	246,407	6.4
Portland, Ore.	85,964	550,396	6.4
Atlanta	84,316	519,145	6.2
Milwaukee/Milwaukee County[a]	154,880	953,328	6.2
Toledo	51,597	316,851	6.1
San Diego	207,575	1,266,731	6.1
Arlington, Tex.	61,322	371,038	6.1
Denver	98,142	588,349	6.0
Houston	370,818	2,208,180	6.0
Riverside, Calif.	49,920	294,437	5.9
Dallas	219,223	1,266,372	5.8
Omaha	74,048	424,482	5.7
Mesa	79,990	452,933	5.7
Plano	46,080	260,796	5.7
Columbus	134,568	747,755	5.6
Lincoln	48,000	248,744	5.2
Phoenix	303,907	1,552,259	5.1
Raleigh	73,600	375,806	5.1
San Antonio	260,832	1,328,984	5.1
Fort Wayne	50,560	251,247	5.0
Henderson, Nev.	51,200	249,386	4.9
Tampa	71,720	336,823	4.7
Low-Density Cities			
Austin	160,969	743,074	4.6
Albuquerque	115,608	518,271	4.5
Bakersfield	72,320	315,837	4.4
Tucson	124,588	525,529	4.2
Wichita	86,879	361,420	4.2
El Paso	159,405	606,913	3.8
Memphis	178,761	674,028	3.8
Greensboro, N.C.	66,560	247,183	3.7
Fort Worth	187,222	681,818	3.6
Indianapolis	231,342	795,458	3.4
Aurora, Colo.	90,880	311,794	3.4
Tulsa	116,891	384,037	3.3
Colorado Springs	118,874	376,427	3.2
Louisville	246,400	713,877	2.9
Corpus Christi	99,200	285,507	2.9
Virginia Beach	158,903	434,743	2.7

continued

City	Area (acres)	Population (2007)	Population Density (persons per acre)
Charlotte/Mecklenburg[a]	337,280	890,515	2.6
Kansas City, Mo.	200,664	475,830	2.4
Honolulu/Honolulu County[a]	384,000	905,034	2.4
Nashville/Davidson	321,280	590,807	1.8
Lexington/Fayette	182,400	282,114	1.5
Jacksonville	537,000	805,605	1.5
Oklahoma City	388,463	547,274	1.4
Anchorage/Anchorage Borough[a]	1,258,880	279,671	0.2
Median, all cities			6.0

[a]Because park agency operates on a countywide basis, population and acreage are for the entire county.
Source: Center for City Park Excellence, The Trust for Public Land

Appendix 2

Acres of Parkland per 1,000 Persons, Largest Cities

City	Population (2007)	Park Acres	Acres per 1,000
High-Density Cities			
Washington, D.C.	588,292	7,617	12.9
Boston	608,352	5,040	8.3
Baltimore	640,150	4,905	7.7
Philadelphia	1,449,634	10,886	7.5
San Francisco	764,976	5,384	7.0
Long Beach	466,520	3,275	7.0
Jersey City	242,389	1,660	6.8
Los Angeles	3,834,340	23,761	6.2
New York	8,310,212	38,229	4.6
Chicago	2,836,658	11,860	4.2
Newark, N.J.	280,135	822	2.9
Miami	424,662	955	2.2
Santa Ana, Calif.	339,555	357	1.1
Median, High-Density Cities			6.8
Intermediate High-Density Cities			
St. Paul	277,251	5,476	19.8
San Jose	939,899	16,303	17.3
Minneapolis	377,392	5,864	15.5
Oakland	401,489	5,217	13.0
Pittsburgh	311,218	3,122	10.0
St. Louis	355,663	3,381	9.5
Seattle	594,210	5,476	9.2
Buffalo	272,632	2,140	7.8
Cleveland	438,042	3,127	7.1
Detroit	916,952	5,890	6.4
Anaheim	333,249	864	2.6
Stockton	287,245	665	2.3
Median, Intermediate High-Density Cities			9.4

continued

City	Population (2007)	Park Acres	Acres per 1,000
Intermediate Low-Density Cities			
San Diego	1,266,731	45,492	35.9
Raleigh	375,806	12,252	32.6
Phoenix	1,552,259	41,980	27.0
Portland, Ore.	550,396	13,480	24.5
Lincoln	248,744	5,945	23.9
Houston	2,208,180	52,739	23.9
Dallas	1,266,372	29,401	23.2
Omaha	424,482	9,560	22.5
San Antonio	1,328,984	27,922	21.0
Cincinnati	332,458	6,817	20.5
Columbus	747,755	14,360	19.2
Plano	260,796	4,555	17.5
Milwaukee/Milwaukee County[a]	953,328	15,032	15.8
Riverside, Calif.	294,437	4,450	15.1
Sacramento	460,242	5,811	12.6
Arlington, Tex.	371,038	4,681	12.6
St. Petersburg	246,407	2,963	12.0
Denver	588,349	5,900	10.0
Tampa	336,823	3,363	10.0
Fort Wayne	251,247	2,400	9.6
Glendale, Ariz.	253,152	2,159	8.5
Henderson, Nev.	249,386	2,013	8.1
Atlanta	519,145	3,846	7.4
Las Vegas	558,880	4,040	7.2
Toledo	316,851	2,206	7.0
Chandler, Ariz.	246,399	1,554	6.3
Mesa	452,933	2,619	5.8
Fresno	470,508	1,507	3.2
Median, Intermediate Low-Density Cities			13.9
Low-Density Cities			
Anchorage/Anchorage Borough[a]	279,671	501,725	1794.0
Albuquerque	518,271	34,630	66.8
Jacksonville	805,605	46,241	57.4
El Paso	606,913	27,289	45.0
Virginia Beach	434,743	17,853	41.1
Kansas City, Mo.	475,830	17,272	36.3
Austin	743,074	26,271	35.4
Aurora, Colo.	311,794	8,503	27.3

continued

Appendix 2, continued

City	Population (2007)	Park Acres	Acres per 1,000
Colorado Springs	376,427	10,237	27.2
Oklahoma City	547,274	14,684	26.8
Bakersfield	315,837	8,345	26.4
Greensboro, N.C.	247,183	6,167	24.9
Louisville	713,877	15,902	22.3
Lexington/Fayette[a]	282,114	5,840	20.7
Charlotte/Mecklenburg[a]	890,515	17,982	20.2
Tulsa	384,037	7,336	19.1
Nashville/Davidson[a]	590,807	10,392	17.6
Fort Worth	681,818	10,923	16.0
Indianapolis	795,458	11,137	14.0
Memphis	674,028	9,140	13.6
Wichita	361,420	4,458	12.3
Corpus Christi	285,507	2,024	7.1
Tucson	525,529	3,658	7.0
Honolulu/Honolulu County[a]	905,034	6,255	6.9
Median, Low-Density Cities			23.6
Median, all cities			12.9

Note: Park acreage includes only parkland within city limits.
[a] Because park agency operates on a countywide basis, population and acreage are for the entire county.
Source: Center for City Park Excellence, The Trust for Public Land

Appendix 3

Parkland as a Percent of City Area, Largest Cities

City	City Area (acres)	Park Acres	Percent
High-Density Cities			
New York	195,072	38,229	19.6%
Washington, D.C.	39,297	7,617	19.4
San Francisco	29,884	5,384	18.0
Jersey City	9,600	1,660	17.3
Boston	30,992	5,040	16.3
Philadelphia	86,456	10,886	12.6
Long Beach	32,281	3,275	10.1
Baltimore	51,714	4,905	9.5
Chicago	145,362	11,860	8.2
Los Angeles	300,201	23,761	7.9
Newark, N.J.	15,360	822	5.4
Miami	22,830	955	4.2
Santa Ana, Calif.	17,280	357	2.1
Median, High-Density Cities			10.1%
Intermediate High-Density Cities			
Minneapolis	35,130	5,864	16.7%
St. Paul	33,920	5,476	16.1
San Jose	111,910	16,303	14.6
Oakland	35,875	5,217	14.5
Seattle	53,677	5,476	10.2
Pittsburgh	35,573	3,122	8.8
St. Louis	39,630	3,381	8.5
Buffalo	26,240	2,140	8.2
Detroit	88,810	5,890	6.6
Cleveland	49,650	3,127	6.3
Anaheim	31,360	864	2.8
Stockton	35,200	665	1.9
Median, Intermediate High-Density Cities			8.7%

continued

Appendix 3, continued

City	City Area (acres)	Park Acres	Percent
Intermediate Low-Density Cities			
San Diego	207,575	45,492	21.9%
Raleigh	73,600	12,252	16.6
Portland, Ore.	85,964	13,480	15.7
Houston	370,818	52,739	14.2
Phoenix	303,907	41,980	13.8
Cincinnati	49,898	6,817	13.7
Dallas	219,223	29,401	13.4
Omaha	74,048	9,560	12.9
Lincoln	48,000	5,945	12.4
Columbus	134,568	14,360	10.7
San Antonio	260,832	27,922	10.7
Plano	46,080	4,555	9.9
Milwaukee/Milwaukee County	154,880	15,032	9.7
Sacramento	62,180	5,811	9.3
Riverside, Calif.	49,920	4,450	8.9
St. Petersburg	38,400	2,963	7.7
Arlington, Tex.	61,322	4,681	7.6
Glendale, Ariz.	35,840	2,159	6.0
Denver	98,142	5,900	6.0
Las Vegas	72,514	4,040	5.6
Fort Wayne	50,560	2,400	4.7
Tampa	71,720	3,363	4.7
Atlanta	84,316	3,846	4.6
Toledo	51,597	2,206	4.3
Chandler, Ariz.	36,480	1,554	4.3
Henderson, Nev.	51,200	2,013	3.9
Mesa	79,990	2,619	3.3
Fresno	66,791	1,507	2.3
Median, Intermediate Low-Density Cities			**9.1%**
Low-Density Cities			
Anchorage/Anchorage Borough	1,258,880	501,725	39.9%
Albuquerque	115,608	34,630	30.0
El Paso	159,405	27,289	17.1
Austin	160,969	26,271	16.3
Bakersfield	72,320	8,345	11.5
Virginia Beach	158,903	17,853	11.2
Aurora, Colo.	90,880	8,503	9.4
Greensboro, N.C.	66,560	6,167	9.3
Jacksonville	537,000	46,241	8.6

continued

City	City Area (acres)	Park Acres	Percent
Colorado Springs	118,874	10,237	8.6%
Kansas City, Mo.	200,664	17,272	8.6
Louisville	246,400	15,902	6.5
Tulsa	116,891	7,336	6.3
Fort Worth	187,222	10,923	5.8
Charlotte/Mecklenburg[a]	337,280	17,982	5.3
Wichita	86,879	4,458	5.1
Memphis	178,761	9,140	5.1
Indianapolis	231,342	11,137	4.8
Oklahoma City	388,463	14,684	3.8
Nashville/Davidson	321,280	10,392	3.2
Lexington/Fayette	182,400	5,840	3.2
Tucson	124,588	3,658	2.9
Corpus Christi	99,200	2,024	2.0
Honolulu/Honolulu County[a]	384,000	6,255	1.6
Median, Low-Density Cities			6.4%
Median, all cities			8.6%

[a] Because park agency operates on a countywide basis, population and acreage are for the entire county.

Source: Center for City Park Excellence, The Trust for Public Land.

Appendix 4

Spending per Resident on Parks and Recreation, Largest Cities Fiscal Year 2007

City	Population (2007)	Total Spending on Parks and Recreation	Spending per Resident
San Francisco	764,976	$229,205,252	$300
Chandler, Ariz.	246,399	68,808,216	279
Washington, D.C.	588,292	162,812,759	277
Seattle	594,210	153,820,707	259
Minneapolis	377,392	80,668,798	214
St. Paul	277,251	57,363,000	207
Las Vegas	558,880	108,179,909	194
Plano	260,796	50,419,735	193
Phoenix	1,552,259	248,996,357	160
Portland, Ore.	550,396	86,650,852	157
Tampa	336,823	48,471,613	144
Long Beach	466,520	66,780,528	143
Kansas City, Mo.	475,830	67,561,173	142
New York	8,310,212	1,177,104,326	142
Cincinnati	332,458	46,850,958	141
Henderson	249,386	33,761,451	135
Aurora, Colo.	311,794	42,112,518	135
Virginia Beach	434,743	56,466,263	130
Chicago	2,836,658	358,252,749	126
Raleigh	375,806	47,411,648	126
San Diego	1,266,731	156,695,266	124
Denver	588,349	71,599,358	122
Nashville/Davidson	590,807	67,248,633	114
Atlanta	519,145	59,044,936	114
Sacramento	460,242	52,205,273	113
Dallas	1,266,372	141,559,252	112
San Jose	939,899	100,539,980	107
Bakersfield	315,837	33,666,719	107
Riverside, Calif.	294,437	30,821,956	105
Honolulu/Honolulu County	905,034	92,372,263	102
Boston	608,352	61,298,456	101
Colorado Springs	376,427	34,975,829	93
Tucson	525,529	48,439,933	92
Oakland	401,489	36,639,244	91
Greensboro, N.C.	247,183	22,209,667	90
Anaheim	333,249	27,745,975	83

continued

City	Population (2007)	Total Spending on Parks and Recreation	Spending per Resident
Austin	743,074	$61,604,662	$83
Columbus	747,755	61,385,891	82
St. Petersburg	246,407	20,082,395	82
Cleveland	438,042	35,137,313	80
Anchorage/Anchorage Borough	279,671	22,197,245	79
Glendale, Ariz.	253,152	19,215,299	76
Jersey City	242,389	18,343,171	76
San Antonio	1,328,984	99,632,176	75
Corpus Christi	285,507	21,368,893	75
Lexington/Fayette	282,114	19,484,199	69
Charlotte/Mecklenburg	890,515	61,363,894	69
Lincoln	248,744	17,096,796	69
Arlington, Tex.	371,038	25,416,070	68
Philadelphia	1,449,634	98,705,892	68
Baltimore	640,150	43,230,406	68
Miami	424,662	27,566,438	65
Newark, N.J.	280,135	17,969,407	64
St. Louis	355,663	22,362,534	63
Fort Worth	681,818	42,357,188	62
Mesa	452,933	27,526,395	61
Albuquerque	518,271	31,382,000	61
Milwaukee/Milwaukee County	953,328	55,641,698	58
Wichita	361,420	20,532,393	57
Jacksonville	805,605	45,553,307	57
Pittsburgh	311,218	17,179,649	55
Fort Wayne	251,247	13,858,649	55
Louisville	713,877	39,237,621	55
Fresno	470,508	25,171,985	53
Oklahoma City	547,274	28,720,717	52
Omaha	424,482	22,228,306	52
Los Angeles	3,834,340	181,577,119	47
Indianapolis	795,458	35,532,390	45
Santa Ana, Calif.	339,555	15,059,729	44
Tulsa	384,037	16,705,961	44
Detroit	916,952	36,500,000	40
Houston	2,208,180	87,457,300	40
Memphis	674,028	26,291,152	39
Toledo	316,851	11,923,351	38
El Paso	606,913	18,612,864	31
Stockton	287,245	6,600,000	23
Buffalo	272,632	3,203,862	12
Total and Median		$5,729,777,869	$82

Note: Total spending includes programming, maintenance, and capital.

Index

Note: Tables and photos are indicated by "t" and "p" after the page number, respectively.